Alesis Fusion PowerStart Guide

by Rich Menga

Original release: 2007
Revised: 2019

https://menga.net

I0425550

Table of Contents

ALESIS FUSION POWERSTART GUIDE

Introduction (2019)

This is a revised re-release of this book. It was originally written in 2007, which at the time of this writing was was 12 years ago.

Please be aware of two things when reading through this book:

First, certain web site links mentioned in this book that were online in 2007 are now no longer available. However, I have included a chapter that includes updated links for places that are online as of 2019 for everything I could find.

Second, in 2007, everyone including myself using a PC was running the Microsoft Windows XP operating system, as that was the current Windows of the time. Most of what's mentioned in this book concerning the XP operating system will still work with Windows 10.

If you are a Fusion owner, you know the synth is old. The Alesis Fusion at this point is considered to be a vintage synthesizer workstation. Even so, **the information presented in this book is historically valuable and still works**. It will help you along with getting up and running with the Fusion if you are new to the workstation.

Enjoy!

Introduction (Original)

The Alesis Fusion synthesizer workstation is undoubtedly one of the best values for the money. It has the features, the ease of use and the power to make music composing and recording easy and fun. If you bought this book, you already know how great the Fusion is. With the information presented here, your Fusion will be even easier to use.

This book does not cover all the features on the Fusion. You should use the information presented here as a complement to the existing Alesis Fusion Reference Manual and Addendum, and not as a primary manual. In basic terms, you can think of this book as a Quick Start Guide on steroids.

You can download the Alesis Fusion Reference Manual as a free download from http://www.alesis.com.

Some thank you notes to:

- Alesis Corporation (http://www.alesis.com)
- Hollow Sun (http://www.hollowsun.com)
- Fusion Club Message Board (http://fusioneer.proboards102.com)

You guys have all been wonderful in producing great products while providing a great sense of community!

The names of the products, software and motion picture titles used in this book belong to their respective trademark and tradename owners and are used to the benefit of said owners with absolutely no intention of infringement.

Copyright ©2007 Rich Menga, Jr.

Web: https://www.menga.net

E-Mail: contactrich@menga.net

About me, Rich Menga, the author of this book

In my style of synthesizer playing and programming, I like to have everything done on the synthesizer itself. I do not use external sequencers or connect to any other devices. Also, I prefer to do things in a way that allows me to compose as fast as possible without having to go to the manual every few minutes just to figure out what I want to do.

In addition to musicianship and home studio prowess, I have many years of experience writing technical documentation in "Plain English" format – meaning that I write documentation that can be followed with very little effort in an easy-to-understand format.

When it comes to synthesizer workstations, I believe in having the workstation itself perform as much as it can without the need to tie in external units, such as external sequencers, controllers and the like. While it's true the Fusion very easily connects to external devices – I prefer the "island unto itself" model of composing, because that's what a workstation synth is designed to do.

Why did I write this book?

I wrote this because while the existing Fusion documentation is thorough, this book covers things that are only available in scattered bits and pieces on the Internet, such as using the Fusion Converter, how to install Hollow Sun sound packs, how to uninstall Hollow Sun sound packs, and so on. It was my goal to centralize this information in one place that can be easily referred back to at any time. It is my hope that you find the information presented here useful that you can use time and time again, and moreover allow music making with the Fusion to be even easier than it already is.

Where to get information on Rich Menga and hear some Fusion music right now

- www.menga.net – My personal site containing my blog, photos and other good stuff.

The power of using free software

This entire book was written using the freely
available OpenOffice suite, available at
http://www.openoffice.org. If the price of that other
office suite has got you down, don't worry.
OpenOffice won't cost you a dime. Runs on
Windows, Macintosh and Linux.

Try it. You'll like it.

A quick glossary of terms

BUTTON

Any button on the Fusion that has printed letters on it, such as PROGRAM, SONG, GLOBAL and so on.

SOFT BUTTON

These are the small round buttons to the left and right of the back-lit display in the middle of the Fusion. These buttons perform different functions depending on what menu you have selected. You will get familiar with this as you read through this book.

Here is a screen shot of a Fusion menu:

All the functions on the left and the right are controlled by the small round buttons on either side of the main display. Being that the functions of these buttons change from screen to screen, that is why they are called "soft" buttons. The software determines what a particular button's function is at any given time.

PITCH WHEEL

The wheel used to adjust the pitch of a sound while playing it, located to the extreme far left.

MODULATION (OR "MOD") WHEEL

The wheel located directly directly to the right of the PITCH WHEEL. Used to adjust the programmed modulation setting of a sound.

CONTROL WHEEL

Not to be confused with the PITCH or MOD wheel, the CONTROL WHEEL is located to the right of the main display. It's the only wheel on the Fusion that is a big circle with six buttons surrounding it.

Selecting a sound

The way to select a sound on the Fusion is by doing the following:

1. Press the PROGRAM button (to the left of the main display in the center of the synthesizer).

2. Press one of the square buttons to the right of the main display to select a sound. You can use the button that states the kind of sound you would like. For example, A is Piano. Then by pressing one of the numbered buttons below A, you select a specific type of piano. If you are currently on ROM: PRESET 1, A 1 is "Holy Grail Grand Piano".

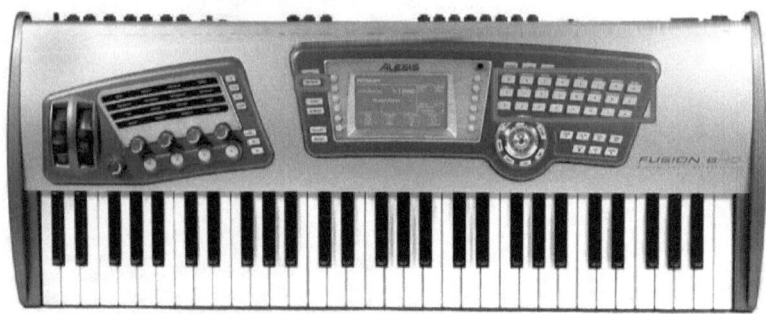

Above: Press PROGRAM button to the left of the main display, then select a sound using the sound selector buttons to the right of the main display.

Using Banks

The Fusion comes installed with several banks of
sounds, such as ROM: PRESET 1, 2, 3, 4,
ELECTRONICA and others. To navigate from bank
to bank, use the BANK left and right buttons located
above the sound selection buttons. By default, the
Fusion is set to bank ROM: PRESET 1. When you
change banks, the display will indicate what bank
you currently have selected.

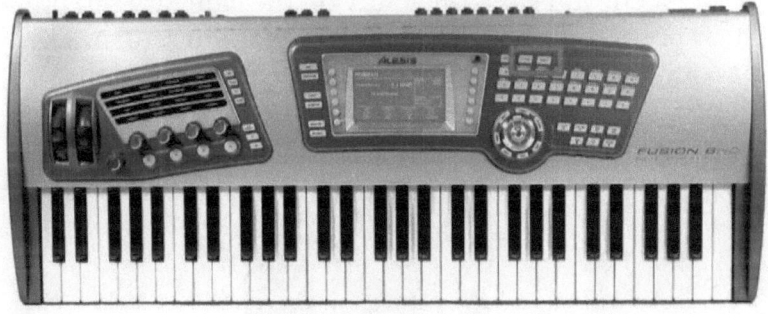

*Above: Use the BANK buttons to navigate through
sound banks.*

Selecting a sound by category

To the left of the BANK buttons is the CATEGORY
button. Press this button to view all available sounds
in an easy-to-use category style.

To navigate different categories and sounds, you can
opt to use the control wheel or the PREV, NEXT,

DEC and INC buttons around the control wheel.

To select a category, rotate the control wheel clockwise to go forward a category and counterclockwise to go back a category. You can also use the INC button and DEC buttons below the control wheel to perform the same function. Once you have selected the category you want, press the NEXT button under the control wheel to select a sound. Use the control wheel or INC and DEC buttons to select the sound you want. When finished, you can either stay on the category screen, or press the PROGRAM button again to return. The sound you have selected will appear on the main program display. To return to category view again, press CATEGORY.

Above: CATEGORY button (top), control wheel and PREV, NEXT, DEC, INC buttons around control wheel (below).

Setting and retrieving Favorites

I find that I use the Favorites function often in the Fusion. It saves me from having to recall certain sounds over and over again.

How Favorites work

What you do when you set Favorites is that you're setting your own bank of sounds from existing sounds. Retrieving a Favorite sound is done through Category view.

How to set a Favorite

1. Pick a sound.

2. Above the control wheel (to the right of the main display), press EDIT.

3. On the main display, press the soft button for Utility (on left of display).

4. On the main display, use the control wheel to highlight 1 → next to Favorite.

5. Press Favorite to save the sound to Favorites 1.

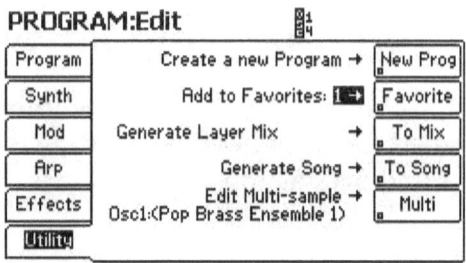

Where it gets confusing (but really isn't)

You can assign multiple sounds to a Favorite. You'll understand what I mean in a moment. For the time being, press PROGRAM, pick a sound different from the one you just had, then add that to Favorites 1. By doing this, you are not overwriting your previous favorite. Rather, you've added an additional sound to Favorite set 1.

Retrieving Favorites

1. Press PROGRAM

2. Press CATEGORY.

3. Use the PREV button under the control wheel to highlight a category.

4. Use the INC button (or rotate the control wheel clockwise) to scroll down to Fav 1. You will see that both sounds you saved to Favorite 1 are listed there.

Removing a Favorite

1. Select a sound from a Favorite that you want to remove.

2. Press EDIT (above the control wheel).

3. Press the soft button on the main display marked Utility.

4. You will notice next to Favorite, it states "Remove from Favorites". Press the soft button for Favorite to remove it.

Assigning different sets of favorites

1. Set a Favorite as you normally would (see previous section on how to add Favorites if you are unfamiliar how to do this).

2. Before pressing the soft button for Favorite to save, press the INC button or rotate the control wheel clockwise to select a different set. You can select 1 through 8.

3. Once you have the set number you want, press the soft button for Favorite to save.

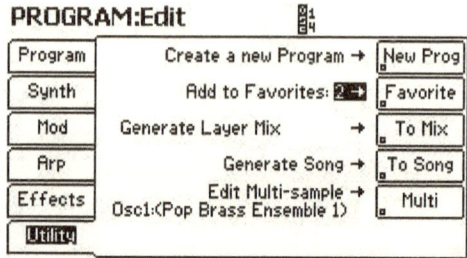

Above: Note that it displays Add to Favorites: 2.

This was done by using the INC button to select that Favorite set.

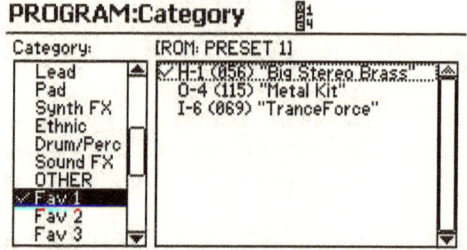

Above: Selecting Favorites 1 from Category view. In this example I have saved three sounds.

If I had added a sound to Favorites: 2, the sound would appear under Fav 2.

Installing different sounds from Hollow Sun

Hollow Sun (http://www.hollowsun.com) is a web site where you can download and install many different sounds aside from the stock banks that come with the Fusion.

Assumptions

The following documentation assumes you are using a computer using the Microsoft Windows XP operating system, equipped with hi-speed USB 2.0 ports. The vast majority of computers built from 2002 to present have hi-speed USB ports, so if your computer was manufactured after 2003, you most likely have them already.

Note to Macintosh users: It is possible to also do this with a Mac since USB is a universal format that can be recognized in both Windows and Macintosh computers.

Things you will need

- A CF (CompactFlash) card installed in the Fusion. There is a CF slot in the back. It is suggested you purchase a CF card that has at least 256MB of available memory on it.

- A USB cable that connects the Fusion to your home computer.

- A program on your computer that extract ZIP files with proper directory recreation. I suggest using WinZIP (http://www.winzip.com) if you are using a computer with Microsoft Windows.

Quick note: You may ask "Couldn't I just place the appropriate sounds directly on the Fusion's hard drive?" Yes, you could. However, to avoid anyone accidentally erasing information from the Fusion's hard drive, it is best to use a CF card first. By doing this, if you make a mistake, you can try again without fear of losing any data.

Installing and formatting your CF Card

If you have a brand new CF card installed in the Fusion, you should do this first before anything else.

IMPORTANT NOTE: Follow this instructions SLOWLY and CAREFULLY so you do not format your Fusion's hard drive accidentally.

1. Turn OFF the Fusion.

2. Insert the CF card in the slot located in the back of the Fusion.

3. Turn ON the Fusion. Wait until boot process completes.

4. Press GLOBAL.

5. Press the soft button labeled Media.

6. Using the control wheel or INC and DEC
   buttons, highlight your CF card. It should
   look like this:

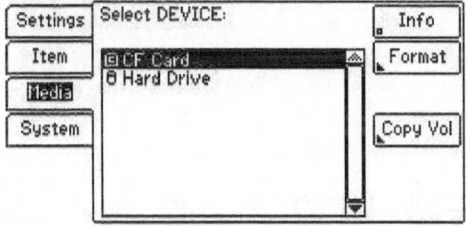

7. Once you are ABSOLUTELY SURE that the
   CF card is highlighted, press the soft button
   labeled Format. The CF card will then be
   formatted.

**"Why do I need to do this? Isn't the CF card
already blank since it's new?"**

The Fusion uses a specific directory structure that
must exist in order for sounds to be placed on it.
Without the directory structure, any sounds places
on it will not work. Instructing the Fusion to format
the CF card will create the proper directory
structure.

Download and extract the sounds from hollowsun.com

Download HS_Freepack_01.zip from
http://www.hollowsun.com/downloads

Use WinZIP to open that file. It should look something like this:

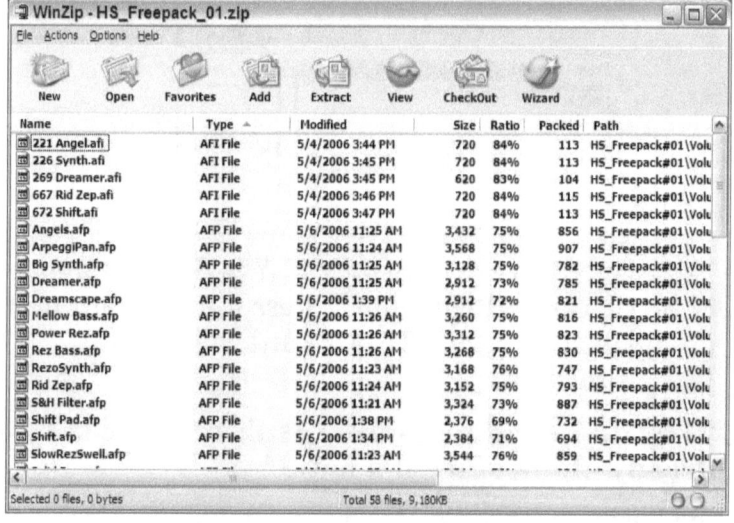

Press the button in WinZIP labeled **Extract**. It should look similar to this:

At the top left, type in c:\hollowsun

At the bottom left, check the option for **Use folder names**

Click Extract at the top right. All files in the ZIP will extract to C:\HOLLOWSUN\HS_Freepack#01

Close WinZIP.

Send the sounds to the Fusion

Now that we've downloaded the sounds and extracted to the hard drive, we can send these sounds to the Fusion itself.

Plug in the USB cable to the back of the Fusion.

Plug in the USB cable to your computer. Your Fusion's display should now read:

USB File Transfer Mode

Fusion is connected as USB Hi-Speed device.

You may now transfer files between the Fusion and the computer through USB.

To exit this mode, dismount the Fusion drives from your computer first, and then unplug the USB cable.

IMPORTANT NOTE: If you've never plugged the Fusion into your computer before, it may take anywhere from one to two minutes for your computer to recognize it and enable it for transfer. NO DRIVERS ARE NECESSARY. Your computer will auto-detect appropriately.

In Windows Explorer (in Windows: Start Button, All Programs, Accessories, Windows Explorer), you will note that two new drive letters have appeared. One for your Fusion's hard drive, the other for the Fusions installed CF card. It should look something like the illustration below.

(Note: Your drives may be assigned different letters. On my computer they were assigned E and G.)

When you expand your CF card's folder, it should have a directory structure like the illustration below. IF IT DOES NOT, you will need to reformat the CF Card again via the Fusion.

Navigate to your hollowsun folder that you created on drive C earlier. Expand it, and it should look like this:

SINGLE RIGHT CLICK "Volume".

A menu will appear. SINGLE LEFT CLICK "Copy" to copy the folder.

Navigate to your CF card's drive letter.

SINGLE RIGHT CLICK the DRIVE LETTER ITSELF.

A menu will appear. SINGLE LEFT CLICK "Paste".

You will receive a warning that will look like this:

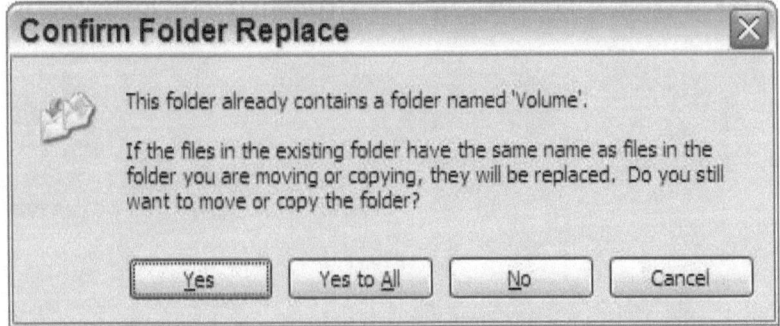

Click "Yes to All". The contents will be copied to the Fusion's CF Card.

Next to your clock in Windows XP, there will be a small icon that looks like the image below. DOUBLE-LEFT-CLICK this icon.

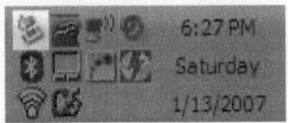

A window will appear. Select **USB Mass Storage Device**, then click Stop. See image below for example.

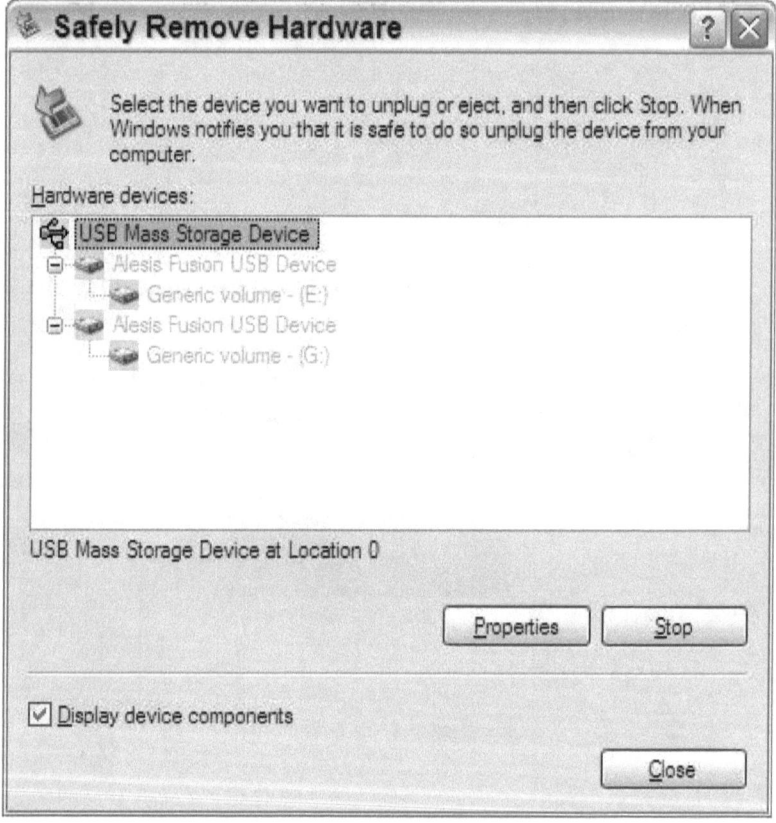

Another window will appear. Click OK. See image below for example.

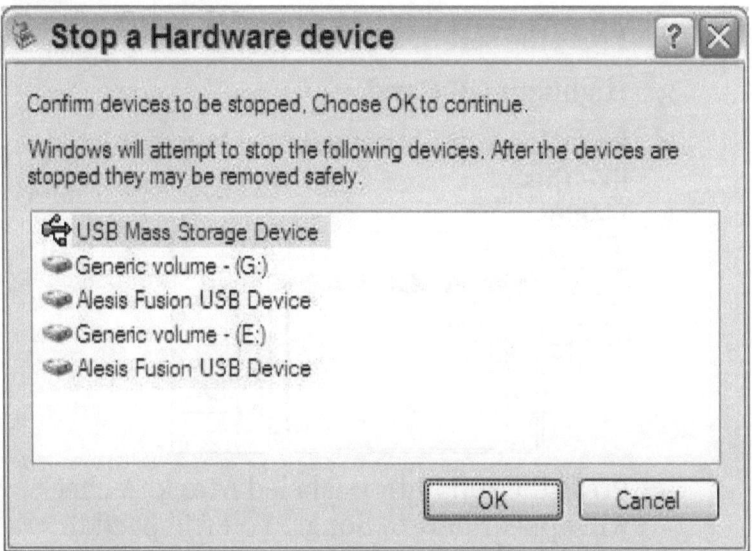

The following notice will appear:

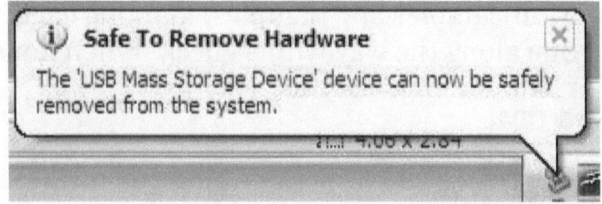

You can now safely unplug the Fusion's USB cable from the Fusion itself and your computer.

You're almost done...

At this point, the Fusion needs to index the new

sounds that have be sent to it. This is easy.

1. Press **GLOBAL**.

2. Press the soft button labeled **Media**.

3. Highlight **CF Card**.

4. Press the soft button marked **Item**. It looks like this:

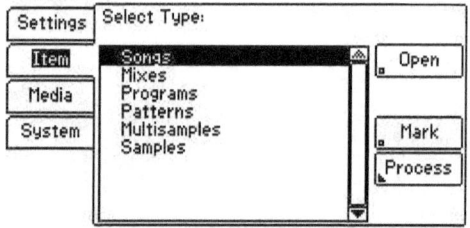

5. Press the soft button labeled **Mark**. A check will appear next to Songs. You will need to use the INC and DEC buttons (or control wheel) to select Mixes, Programs, Patterns, Multisamples and Samples, marking each one along the way with a check. When done, it should look like this:

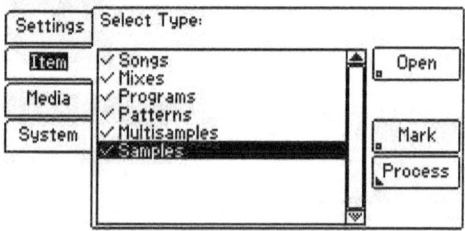

6. When finished, press the soft button labeled **Process**.

7. On the next screen, press the soft button labeled **Verify**.

8. On the next screen, press the soft button labeled **Yes**. The Fusion will report that everything has been verified.

Selecting a new sound from what you just verified

1. Press PROGRAM.

2. Press the right BANK button, and continue to press it until the main display looks like this:

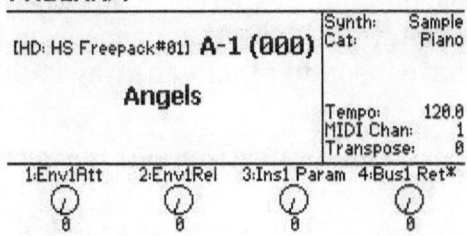

Success! You now have HS Freepack#01 installed on your Fusion!

Using the sequencer the easy way

The sequencer, once properly learned, is very easy to work with. Here are my recommendations for the fastest easiest use of the internal sequencer without the need for any external devices.

Importing a sound to the sequencer along with its effects

The easiest way to start a sequence is to pick a sound you like and go from there. Note: You don't have to do this, but in my experience, I play around with a sound first, then make a sequence from there, and I like to have it sound exactly the way it did in Program mode.

Pick a sound. I've chosen ROM: Preset 2 A-6 "Wurly Velo"

PROGRAM

		Synth:	Sample
[ROM: PRESET 2]	A-6 (005)	Cat:	Piano
	Wurly Velo		
		Tempo:	120.0
		MIDI Chan:	1
		Transpose:	0

1:Ins1 Param* 2:Ins1 Param 3:Bus2 Send 4:Bus1 Send*

Press the EDIT button above the control wheel (on

the right side).

Press the soft button marked Utility.

Press the soft button marked **To Song**. (Note: If
you receive a warning that states *Creating/Selecting
a new song will lose all changes made to the
current song. Do you want to store the changes?*,
you can opt to save the current sequence loaded by
pressing the soft button for Yes, or select No to
discard.)

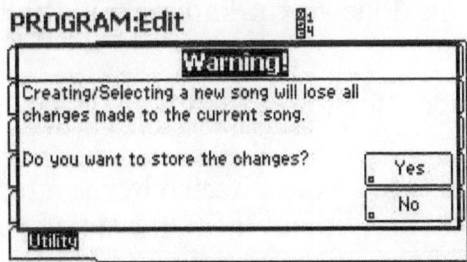

Press the EDIT button above the control wheel.

Press the soft button labeled Track.

Press the soft button labeled Output.

Use your PREV and NEXT buttons around the control wheel to highlight the check box for Use Prog Value.

Use the INC and DEC buttons around the control wheel to place a check in the Use Prog Value checkbox.

```
SONG:Edit  001:01.000

 Song    | EDIT Track:        Trk 1(of 1)  | General
         | Volume:                  100%
 Track   |    Use Prog value:                Range
         | Pan:              Center
 Editor  |    Use Prog value:                Param
         | Insert: (Overdrive Rotary)    1
 Arp     | Bus Send 1:               30%   | Controls
         |  (Plate Reverb)
 Effects | Bus Send 2:               13%   | Output
         |  (Multi Chorus HP)
 Utility | Dry Level:               100%   | Jump FX
         | Output Bus:              Main
```

By doing this, the sound you just sent to the sequencer sounds identical to the way it did in Program view, with the exception of any modifications done via the knobs about the T-buttons.

Reasons you would place a sound in the sequencer this way:

Some sounds are greatly affected by the effects applied to them. Without them, the sound you get may be "flat" and not to your liking.

More often than not, you will be experimenting with a sound and want to create a song from it. In this instance, it is best to place the sound in the sequencer exactly as you originally heard it in

Program view.

Do you have to place a sound in the sequencer like this? No. It's optional.

Creating and composing a simple song

Creating a new song

Note: If you created a new song by importing a sound directly to the sequencer in the previous section, you can skip this step, however, it's recommended you do this anyway just to learn how it's done. It's very easy.

1. Press the SONG button.

2. Press the EDIT button above the control wheel.

3. Press the soft button labeled Utility.

4. Press the soft button labeled New Song.

5. You may receive this warning below. Select Yes to save or No to discard. If you don't have anything worth saving in the sequencer currently, just select No.

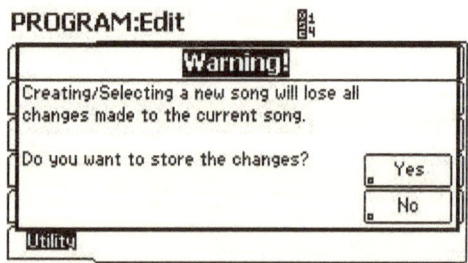

A new empty song has now been created.

Adjusting tempo

1. Press the SONG button.

2. Press the EDIT button.

3. Press the soft button labeled Song (not to be confused with the regular SONG button– this one is on your display!)

4. Press the soft button labeled General.

5. Use your PREV and NEXT buttons around the control wheel to highlight the tempo, which is by default set to 120.0 BPM (beats per minute).

6. Once the tempo is highlighted, use the control wheel or the INC and DEC buttons to adjust the tempo. Note that as you speed up or slow down the tempo, the flashing amber TEMPO light (to the left of the main display) flashes in time to what you set the tempo to.

Any adjustment to the tempo is applied immediately.

Enabling/Disabling automatic quantize

One of the very nice features of the Fusion is its ability to quantize as you record. What this means is that if you're not so good at keeping things in time as you record them, the Fusion will assist you if you want it to.

While some may think this is a wonderful feature, others may find it very annoying and want to manually quantize if need be at a later time (covered later in this book).

This is how you enable or disable the automatic quantize.

1. Press the SONG button.

2. Press the EDIT button.

3. Press the soft button labeled Record.

4. Use the control wheel or PREV and NEXT buttons to highlight the field next to Quantize.

5. Use the control wheel or the INC and DEC

buttons to modify this setting. If you want to turn the auto-quantize OFF, press DEC until the setting reads Off.

A few notes on quantizing as you record

Where most would find this useful is when they are recording things that require strict timing, such as drums, techno bass tracks, and so on.

There are many levels of quantizing. The settings that most would find useful are 8th note and 16th note.

How quantizing works:

A sequence by default is set to 4/4 @ 120bpm. If, for example, you set Quantize to Quarter-note , the Fusion will only allow four notes per measure. If set to 8th note, the Fusion allows eight notes per measure. If set to 16th note, the Fusion allows for sixteen notes per measure, and so on.

Quantizing purposely limits the number of notes heard on playback in order to keep them in time.

If you notice that notes played are "missing" on playback, consider setting Quantize to Off or to a higher setting (such as from 8th note to 16th note).

Manually quantizing a track is covered lated in this book.

Recording your first sequence

1. Press the SONG button.

2. Press the RECORD button (far right side of Fusion). The RECORD button will light up in red. The PLAY button at this point is blinking, alternating from amber to green.

3. When ready, press PLAY. You will by default be given two countdown measures and hear an audible metronome (also known as a "click track"). The main display will show a negative number leading up to zero, which is when you start playing. Note the large negative number in the illustration below.

4. When finished recording your sequence press the STOP button (next to the PLAY button). All lights turn back to an amber color at this point.

5. You can "rewind" back to zero in one of two ways. You can use the REW button which will go back one measure at a time, or just skip directly to zero by using LOCATE (just above and to the left of STOP).

6. Look on the display to confirm you at at the beginning of your sequence. At the top, it should read 001:01.000. See illustration for example.
(Note: The sound you have selected may be different from below – what is important is the song position at the very top.)

```
SONG:Edit  001:01.000

  Song    EDIT Track:          Trk 1(of 1)     General
  Track   Enable:                    ☑
          Program:        [ROM: PRESET 1]      Range
                                  A-1 (000)
  Editor  Holy Grail Grand Piano              Param
  Arp     Record Arm:             Auto        Controls
          Link:                   None
  Effects Arp Num: 1       MIDI Ch:    1       Output
          Enable Loop:            ☐
  Utility  Loop Start:     001: 01. 000
           Loop End:       001: 01. 000
```

7. Press PLAY. Your song will then be played back to you.

You have successfully created your first sequence!

Note: Later on in this book will be detailed instructions on how to create a more advanced sequence. For the time being, lets store (as in save) our existing sequence, then create a new blank song first.

Storing your song

1. Press the SONG button.

2. Press the STORE button (located around the control wheel). Your display should look similar to the illustration below.

3. Press the soft button labeled Rename so we can title our song. Most likely your song is currently named "New" or "New Song 1". We will change this.

4. Press the soft button labeled Delete until your title is blank. It should look like this.

5. There are two primary ways of naming a song. You can use the INC and DEC buttons around the

control wheel (which I find very time consuming), or you can use the keyboard itself.

The lowest C key is [space], C# is the letter a. If you press C# again, it turns into a capital A. As you go up the keyboard, the letters change appropriately. And yes, black keys do count!

When you want to place spaces between words, OR move back and forth between characters, use the PREV and NEXT buttons around the control wheel.

If you make a mistake and want to delete a character, use the PREV and NEXT buttons to highlight the character, then press the soft button labeled Delete.

Note: THIS DOES TAKE GETTING USED TO. Do not get frustrated if it takes a long time to title your first song.

You can name the song whatever you like, but for this example I have used My first Fusion song, and it looks like this:

6. When finished, press the soft button labeled OK.
Your display should then look like this:

7. Now we select where the song will be saved to. By
default, the song will be saved to the Fusion's
internal hard drive bank, labeled [HD: User]. In
addition, we must select a place for the song which
is currently blank.

Selecting the bank to store to

See the previous illustration, and note that Bank is
set to [HD: User]. You can highlight this with the
PREV and NEXT buttons around the control wheel.
Once highlighted, and if you have a CompactFlash
card installed in your Fusion, you can use the INC
and DEC buttons around the control wheel to select
it. The Bank would then read [CF: User].

It is suggested you save to the internal hard drive
(HD), as it is much larger than a CF card.

Selecting the location to store to

All songs in the Fusion are assigned an internal
designation. See the previous illustration, and note

that the number is set to A-1 (000) "". What you
need to pay attention to is the "". This means that
the current area selected is blank, and ready to save
to. If you try to overwrite an existing song, you will
receive a warning that looks similar to the
illustration below.

(Note: If you've never saved a song to the Fusion,
you won't get this warning – but it's good to know
for later on just in case you run into this situation.)

It is suggested that you do not overwrite. Select the
soft button labeled No, highlight the area under [HD
User] using the PREV and NEXT buttons, and then
use the INC and DEC buttons to locate an area that's
blank.

8. Once you have a bank and location to save to,
press the soft button labeled Store. Your song will
then save.

IMPORTANT NOTE: If you do not save your song
before shutting off the Fusion, YOU WILL LOSE IT.
Always remember to store your song!

Loading a previously saved song

1. Press the GLOBAL button.

2. Press the soft button labeled Item.

3. Using the control wheel or the INC and DEC buttons, highlight Songs. Your screen should look like this:

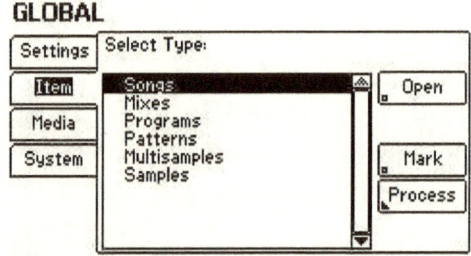

4. Press the soft button labeled Open.

5. If you have a CompactFlash card installed, you
will see two choices for what Song Bank to open;
[CF: User] and [HD: User]. If you do not have a CF
card installed, the only choice will be [HD: User].
Highlight [HD: User] and press the soft button
labeled Open.

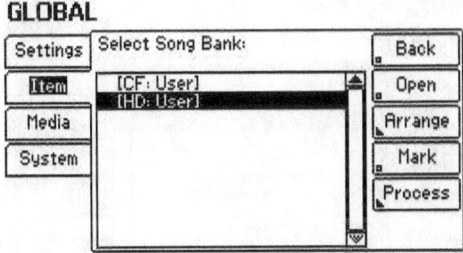

6. Highlight the song you want to load using the control wheel or the INC and DEC buttons. If you have only one song saved, that is the only choice available. If you have multiple songs saved, you can scroll and choose which one you want to load. Here is an illustration of what it looks like when you have multiple songs saved.

Note that the first one is called My ... Fusion song. This is the song we saved a moment ago in the previous section of this book.

7. Press the soft button labeled Open to open the highlighted song. The song will load, and your display should look something like this:

You have successfully loaded a song!

Creating an advanced song with multiple tracks (synth only)

Note: This section does not include synth + audio tracks. That is mentioned later in this book. For the time being, we will concentrate on synth tracks only. It's important to know this before adding external instruments via the multitrack recorder later on.

Create a new song. If you have forgotten how to do this, see instructions for "Creating a Simple Song", then come back here once done.

Adjust settings for track 1

By default, you will be brought to the Track screen in Song mode after a new song is created. The first sound assigned is always "Holy Grail Grand Piano". The screen looks like the illustration below. Note the top of the screen where it states EDIT Track: Trk 1(of 1). This indicates you have a song with one track assigned, and that you are currently editing track #1.

```
SONG:Edit  001:01.000
┌────────┐ EDIT Track:      Trk 1(of 1)  ┌─────────┐
│  Song  │ Enable:               ☑       │ General │
├────────┤ Program:     [ROM: PRESET 1]  ├─────────┤
│ Track  │              A-1 (000)        │  Range  │
├────────┤ Holy Grail Grand Piano        ├─────────┤
│ Editor │                               │  Param  │
├────────┤ Record Arm:            Auto   ├─────────┤
│  Arp   │ Link:                  None   │ Controls│
├────────┤ Arp Num: 1   MIDI Ch:     1   ├─────────┤
│ Effects│ Enable Loop:            ☐     │ Output  │
├────────┤   Loop Start:    001: 01. 000 └─────────┘
│ Utility│   Loop End:      001: 01. 000
└────────┘
```

Let's change this sound to something different. Using the PREV and NEXT buttons around the control wheel, highlight A-1 (000).

Rotate the control wheel clockwise slowly. You will notice you can select different sounds this way.

Use the INC and DEC buttons. You will notice you can also select sounds this way.

Press the B button then the 7 button. You will notice the sound changes to B-7 "Chimey". This is another way of selecting a sound. Quick note: Selecting sounds by category is not possible when selecting a sound in Song mode. If you press the CATEGORY button, the Fusion will state "Category is not available."

If you selected B-7 for track 1, the screen would look like this:

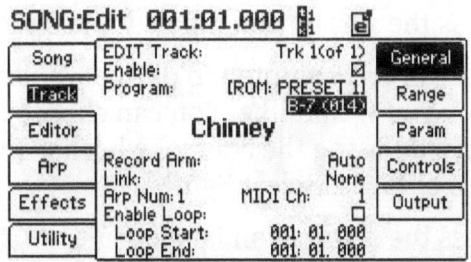

Note: You can switch sound banks easily by using the BANK buttons (next to the CATEGORY

button) if you wish to do so. The default bank is ROM: PRESET 1. If you switch banks, this

will change to ROM: PRESET 2, ROM: PRESET 3 and so on.

Now that we've selected a sound for track 1, let's move on to track 2.

Creating new tracks for your song

1. On the same screen (see previous section), press the soft button labeled Song. Note, this is the soft button, not the regular SONG button.

2. Press the soft button labeled Add Track.

3. You will be prompted to define what type of track you would like. You can choose Synth or Audio using the control wheel or INC and DEC buttons. Select Synth.

4. Press the soft button labeled OK.

Track 2 will be created using the default sound "Holy Grail Grand Piano".

Note: The reason the grand piano is always chosen is because a sound must be selected by the Fusion in order to create a track. A track cannot be defined without a sound. By default, the Fusion will always choose the first sound defined in the system, which is "Holy Grail Grand Piano".

Your screen will now indicate you are on track 2, as
shown by the top which states EDIT Track: Trk 2(of
2). Your screen should look like the illustration
below.

```
SONG:Edit  001:01.000

┌────────┐ EDIT Track:      Trk 2(of 2)  ┌─────────┐
│  Song  │ Enable:                    ☑  │ General │
├────────┤ Program:       [ROM: PRESET 1] ├─────────┤
│ Track  │                  A-1 (000)    │  Range  │
├────────┤                               ├─────────┤
│ Editor │ Holy Grail Grand Piano        │  Param  │
├────────┤ Record Arm:          Auto     ├─────────┤
│  Arp   │ Link:                None     │ Controls│
├────────┤ Arp Num: None  MIDI Ch: Global├─────────┤
│ Effects│ Enable Loop:           ☐      │ Output  │
├────────┤ Loop Start:    001: 01. 000   └─────────┘
│ Utility│ Loop End:      001: 01. 000
└────────┘
```

At this point you now have an empty song with two
empty tracks.

A few words on the Track edit screen

In the last section we took a quick look at the Track edit screen. Here are some more details.

To select a track to edit (such as track 1, track 2 and so on), it is suggested you use your PREV and NEXT buttons around the control wheel. Using the control wheel itself may cause you to accidentally modify a setting you did not want to modify.

While on the Track edit screen, if you have EDIT Track highlighted, you will notice that the tracks which are active are physically lighted by the numbered buttons (to the right of the main display). If track 1 is active, button 1 is lighted in amber. If track 2 is active, button 2 is lighted in amber, and so on. Pressing one of these numbered buttons DOES NOT select a track. Rather, it ENABLES or DISABLES the track. You will notice that if you press a numbered button, the light goes out. That means the track is now disabled. To re-enable it, you must press it again. If a track is disabled, it is synonymous with muting the track, meaning it will not be heard.

Enabling loops (located at the bottom of the Track screen,) DOES NOT loop the song. It only loops the TRACK. Furthermore, it will only loop while you are RECORDING. If you loop a track, then press PLAY, the song will end at its last recorded measure. If you want to loop the entire song, this must be done from the Song menu (SONG, EDIT, Song soft button, General soft button), utilizing the Enable Song Loop function. It works the same way as a track loop, however, it will repeat the song at the points you choose to start and return.

Param, which is a soft button on the right side of the display while viewing the Track edit screen, brings you to a screen where you can adjust the key of whatever sound is assigned to the track you're currently editing. If you want the current track to be played three semitones lower, (from C to A for example), you would set Transpose to -3. IMPORTANT NOTE: If you are editing a DRUM track, transposing is not recommended. You should use Coarse Tune instead, which is directly below Transpose. You can also use Fine Tune as well. If you transpose a drum truck, it will not raise or lower the pitch of the drums. Rather, it will switch the assigned notes (which is what a true transposition is supposed to do), causing unintended results.

Output, which is a soft button on the right side of the display while viewing the Track edit screen, brings you to a screen where you can adjust volume and effects. This section can be very complicated, but it can be best explained like this:

The Fusion uses two main buses to deliver effects. By default, they are set to two types of Reverb (usually "Plate" and "Hall"). Adjusting each one of these settings will give the sound on the currently edited track that effect.

In addition to the buses, you have the ability to assign one of four Inserts. This is an additional effect that can be assigned to the track. An Insert is a SynthIn. They are one and the same.

Quick Insert and SynthIn Tutorial – Adding distortion to a sound

1. Press the SONG button.

2. Press the EDIT button above the control wheel.

3. Press the soft button labeled Track.

4. Select the sound you want to edit by navigating to EDIT Track using your PREV and NEXT buttons around the control wheel, then using INC and DEC to select the track you want to edit.

5. Press the soft button labeled Effects.

6. Press the soft button labeled SynthIns.

7. Note that you are editing SynthIn 1. The screen states EDIT Synth Insert: Insert 1.

8. The default SynthIn selected will normally be 4-band PEQ. Highlight this (if not already highlighted) with your PREV and NEXT buttons around the control wheel.

9. Use the control wheel or your INC and DEC
   buttons to select Stack Drive Distortion.
   NOTE: If you can't find this effect, rotate
   your control wheel counterclockwise until
   you arrive at the first effect, Chorus. Then use
   your INC button to slowly go through each
   effect until you find Stack Drive Distortion.

10. One Stack Drive Distortion is selected, press
    the soft button labeled Settings.

11. Using the PREV and NEXT buttons around
    the control wheel, highlight Drive.

12. Set Drive to 75% using the control wheel.

13. Press the NEXT button until Output Level is
    highlighted.

14. Set Output Level to 75% using the control
    wheel.

15. Press the soft button labeled Track.

16. Press the NEXT button to select Insert.

17. Use the INC and DEC buttons to select 1,
    which as you will notice is now Insert: (Stack
    Drive Distor....)

You have successfully set a custom effect for
SynthIn 1, and assigned it to Track 1!

Adjusting song settings before recording

Adjusting Tempo

1. Press the SONG button.

2. Press the EDIT button.

3. Press the soft button labeled Song.

4. Press the soft button labeled General.

5. Use the PREV and NEXT buttons around the control wheel to highlight 120.0 BPM (the default tempo set for any new song).

6. Adjust tempo using the INC and DEC buttons around the control wheel or rotate the control wheel itself. Your tempo will adjust. Note the blinking amber TEMPO light above the knobs to the left side of the Fusion. It will blink to the speed of the tempo you set.

Enabling or disabling automatic quantizing

1. Repeat steps 1 through 3 above.

2. Press the soft button labeled Record.

3. Use the PREV and NEXT buttons around the control wheel to highlight the field next to Quantize, which may be set to 8th Note, some other value, or Off.

4. Use the INC and DEC buttons around the control wheel or the control wheel itself to set

automatic quantizing. If you want it enabled, it's suggested you use 8th Note or 16th Note. If you want it disabled entirely, set to Off.

Setting the Record Method

The two record methods that most people use are Replace and Overdub. There are more methods available, but these are the two you will use the most.

How it is used: If you record a track, then want to record over it entirely, you would use Replace. If you want to add to an existing track, you would use Overdub.

Replace example: You have recorded a drum track, but made an error when recording, so you want to do it over again. You would use Replace in this instance.

Overdub example: You have recorded a drum track with nothing heard but the hi-hat's. Now you want to add kick drums and snare to the same track without overwriting the hi-hat's. You would use Overdub in this instance.

To set the Record Method

1. Press the SONG button.

2. Press the EDIT button.

3. Press the soft button labeled Song.

4. Press the soft button labeled Record.

5. Use the PREV and NEXT buttons around the control wheel to highlight the field next to Record Method.

6. Use the INC and DEC buttons around the control wheel or the control wheel itself to select Replace or Overdub. Note: By default, any new song created is set to Replace unless you change it.

ALESIS FUSION POWERSTART
GUIDE

Recording your song

Before recording, you will need to select the appropriate track you want to record on.

1. Press the SONG button.

2. Press the EDIT button.

3. Press the soft button labeled Track.

4. Use the PREV and NEXT buttons around the control wheel to highlight the field next to EDIT Track.

5. Use the INC and DEC buttons around the control wheel or the control wheel itself to select Track 1(of 2).

You are now ready to record. Press the RECORD button. It will light up in red. When ready, press the PLAY button. You will be given two countdown measures, then recording will start.

Record eight measures (from 1:01.000 to 9:01.000).

When finished, press STOP, then press the LOCATE and REW (LOCATE, hold, REW, let go) to rewind back to the beginning.

Now we will record on track 2.

1. Repeat steps 1 through 4 above.

2. Use the INC and DEC buttons around the control wheel or the control wheel itself to

select Track 2(of 2).

Press the RECORD button, then PLAY. Two countdown measures will be given, then record track 2. Press STOP when finished, the press LOCATE and REW to go back to the beginning.

Press PLAY. You should hear both tracks that you've just recorded.

Setting locations in a song

As your songs get longer and more complex, you will need to utilize the SET LOC and LOCATE buttons to jump to specific parts of your song when necessary. Here's how to do that.

From the instructions in the previous section, we have just recorded a song that is eight measures in length. We will set a location at measure 4.

1. Press the SONG button.

2. Use the FFWD button to move ahead to measure 4, where your display should read 4:01.000.

3. Press and hold SET LOC.

4. Press A (under the category button).

5. Let go of both buttons.

You have now set the location 4:01.000 in this song to A.

Press LOCATE and REW to rewind back to the beginning of the song so the main display reads the location as 001:01.000.

Press and hold LOCATE. While holding LOCATE, press A, then let go of both buttons.

You will notice that your location has just jumped to 4:01.000.

In the Fusion, you can set up to sixteen different locations in a song (A through P). If you wanted to set a different location you might go to later, such as 8:01.000, you could use the FFWD button to fast forward to that point in the song, then press/hold SET LOC, then B. At this point, A would be 4:01.000 and B would be 8:01.000.

How to execute processes on tracks (quantize)

In this section, I will instruct on how to manually quantize (which is the process) a track. This is one of the Fusion's many process functions, but is somewhat buried. However, you will find it's easy to get to once you do it a few times.

Say that Track 1 is out of time and you want to quantize it to put it in time. The way to do this is as follows:

- Select the track
- Execute the process

Sounds complicated, but it's not.

In the following example, we will quantize track 1 to 8th Note.

1. Press the SONG button.

2. Press the EDIT button.

3. Press the soft button labeled Editor.

4. Using the PREV and NEXT buttons, highlight the box next to track 1.

5. Press INC or rotate the control wheel clockwise to check the box (you would press DEC or rotate the control wheel

counterclockwise to remove the check).

6. Press the soft button labeled Process.

7. By default, the Process field will be highlighted, and will usually be set to Clear. Use the INC and DEC buttons or rotate the control wheel clockwise to change it to Note Quantize.

8. Use the NEXT button to highlight the Edit Start field, and set to 001:01.000 (the beginning of the song). You can move through each field using NEXT and PREV.

9. Use the NEXT button to highlight the Edit End field. If you want to quantize the track for the entire length of the song, highlight the first number and use the control wheel. Rotate it clockwise until the number stops. Where it stops will be the end of the song.

10. When finished, use the NEXT button to highlight the Resolution field.

11. Set the Resolution Field to 8th Note using the NEXT and PREV button or the control wheel.

12. The remaining fields Strength, Swing, Window and Offset can be left as is.

13. Press the soft button labeled Execute.

When finished, your screen will display Notice! Region has been quantized.

Please note that it will take a few times before you get used to the method of doing this. The Fusion is a very advanced musical instrument. Executing processes, while very "computery", is something you can use to your advantage later on when composing music.

Copying and Pasting in the Editor

This section is very similar to the previous one, but instead of quantizing, we will copy and paste, and do this with two tracks instead of just one.

The reason you would use copying and pasting is simple. Most songs are composed as verse, chorus, verse, so it would make sense to create the first verse, then a chorus, then a verse. If the first verse is the same after the chorus, you can simply copy and paste it rather than re-recording it.

And here's how we do that.

Copying a section of a song

1. Create a song with two tracks. Make the song eight measures in length (from 1:01.000 to 9:01.000).

2. Press the SONG button.

3. Press the EDIT button.

4. Press the soft button labeled Editor.

5. Highlight track 1, and check the box.

6. Highlight track 2, and check the box.

7. Press the soft button labeled Process.

8. Select the Process Copy.

9. Set Edit Start to 001:01.000

10. Set Edit End to 009:01.000

11. Notes, Controllers, Aftertouch, Pitch and Other Events should all be set to Included. If they are not, set them to be.

12. Press the soft button labeled Execute.

13. You will receive a notice on your screen that states Notice! Region has been copied. Press the soft button labeled OK.

Pasting the section you just copied

Since we know our song ends at 9:01.000, we will paste our section to at that point.

1. Press the soft button labeled Process.

2. Use your PREV and NEXT buttons to highlight the Process field.

3. Select the Process Paste Over (Note: This will ensure that notes do not "bleed" to the section you are pasting to)

4. Select Edit Start, and set to 009:01.000

5. Set Repetitions to 1 (note: If you want to paste multiple times, set to as many repetitions as you'd like – but for this example, use 1)

6. Press the soft button labeled Execute.

7. You will receive a notice on your screen that states Notice! Region has been pasted. Press the soft button labeled OK.

Reviewing what we've just done

1. Press the SONG button.

2. Press LOCATE and REW to rewind to the beginning of the song.

3. Press PLAY.

If all went well, you should hear your recorded tracks twice. Once for the original time you recorded it, and once again for the pasted region for a total of sixteen measures, ending at 17:01.000 (or at the very end of 16, such as 16:04.478).

Using arps and how to compose a song the super-fast way

One of the Fusion's most powerful ways to compose songs very quickly is by using one or more arpeggios, known as an arp in the Fusion.

What is an arpeggio?

Simply put, an arpeggio is a pattern. When you press and hold a key, the Fusion will play that pattern, then repeat it until you release the key.

How many arps can be used in a single song?

The Fusion allows up to four different arpeggios to be used in any song you create.

Creating a super-quick song using built-in arp's

First we will create a song.

1. Press the SONG button.

2. Press the EDIT button.

3. Press the soft button labeled Utility.

4. Press the soft button labeled New Song. If you receive a warning that your old song will be overwritten, you can opt to save the changes if desired. If not, select No to continue creating your

new song.

5. The default sound assigned to track 1 will be Holy Grail Grand Piano. We will leave this as is. In addition, track 1 has an arp 1 assigned to it. Look at the illustration below. Arp Num is set to 1.

6. The arp, while assigned, is turned off. We will need to enable it. Press the ARP ON/OFF button to enable the arp. This is a button located next to the T4 button on the left side of the Fusion. When you press this button, it will become brighter, indicating it's enabled.

7. Press and hold any key on the Fusion. You will notice that the note played repeats itself over and over again. This is because the arp assigned is Simple Drone. If you press two keys at once, the Fusion will play the first key pressed, then the next, then repeat.

8. We will now change this arp to something that sounds better. On the main display, press the soft button labeled Arp. Your screen will look like this, and show the

default arp selected, Simple Drone.

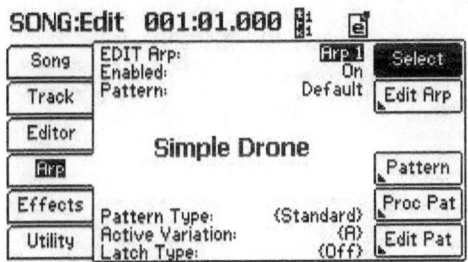

9. Use the PREV and NEXT buttons around the control wheel to highlight the field next to Pattern, which is currently set to Default.

10. Use the INC and DEC buttons or the control wheel to change this setting to ROM: Piano Patterns. (Since we are using a piano sound, it makes sense to use a piano pattern.)

11. Use the PREV and NEXT buttons to highlight A-1 (000), which is the first piano pattern. At this point, your screen should look like this:

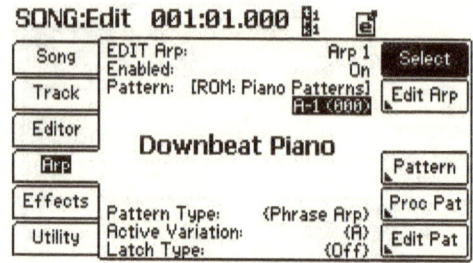

12. Use the INC and DEC buttons around the control wheel or the control wheel itself to change A-1 (000) Downbeat Piano to A-5 (004) R&B EP 4. Your screen should now look like this:

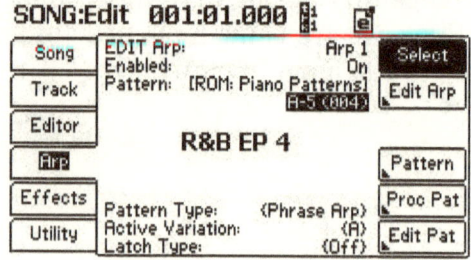

13. Press and hold the middle C key on the Fusion. You will hear a wonderful pattern that sounds much better than Simple Drone!

14. Press the RECORD button.

15. Press the PLAY button.

16. When recording, do nothing but hold the middle C key. Record eight measures.

17. When finished recording, press STOP.

18. Rewind back to the beginning of the song by pressing LOCATE and REW.

19. Press the soft button labeled Song.

20. Press the soft button labeled Add Track.

21. Select the type of track to add as Synth.

22. Press the soft button labeled OK.

23. On the right side of the Fusion, press E then 1 to select Big Fat Upright Bass.

24. You will notice that the Arp Num is set to None. Change this to 2. Your screen should look like this when done:

```
SONG:Edit  001:01.000 ♫¹  [e⁴]
                                  ♫²
┌────────┐ EDIT Track:    Trk 2(of 2) ┌─────────┐
│  Song  │ Enable:             ☑      │ General │
├────────┤ Program:   [ROM: PRESET 1] ├─────────┤
│ Track  │              E-1 (032)     │  Range  │
├────────┤ Big Fat Upright Bass       ├─────────┤
│ Editor │                            │  Param  │
├────────┤ Record Arm:         Auto   ├─────────┤
│  Arp   │ Link:               None   │Controls │
├────────┤ Arp Num:2   MIDI Ch: Global├─────────┤
│ Effects│ Enable Loop:         ☐     │ Output  │
├────────┤ Loop Start:   001: 01. 000 └─────────┘
│ Utility│ Loop End:     001: 01. 000
└────────┘
```

25. Examine the ARP ON/OFF button. If it is dim, press it so it becomes brighter. If it dims when you press it, press it again so it is bright, letting you know it is enabled.

26. Press the middle C key and hold. You should once again hear the Simple Drone arpeggio, just like you did with the piano, except with the bass sound. If you do not hear the Simple Drone arpeggio, check to make sure the ARP ON/OFF button is bright, indicating it is enabled.

27. Press the soft button labeled Arp.

28. Your screen will show you are editing Arp 1. Since we assigned the bass track to Arp 2, we will need edit that specific arp. Use the PREV and NEXT buttons to scroll to the top of the screen, and highlight the field next to EDIT Arp. Change this from Arp 1 to Arp 2.

29. Use the NEXT and PREV buttons to highlight the field next to Pattern.

30. Use the INC and DEC buttons to change Default to ROM: Bass Patterns.

31. Use the NEXT and PREV buttons to higlight A-1 (000).

32. Use the INC and DEC buttons to change this value to D-1 (024) Funk 11.

33. Press and hold the C key before middle C (being this sound is a bass, it is better to play a lower note, but make sure it is a C note). You will hear the pattern play. Release the key when finished.

34. Press RECORD.

35. Press PLAY.

36. Record eight measures of the bass track. Do nothing but hold the C key below middle C.

37. When finished, press STOP.

38. Press LOCATE and REW to rewind back to the beginning of the song.

39. Press the soft button labeled Song.

40. Press the soft button labeled Add Track.

41. Select the type of track to add as Synth, then press the soft button labeled OK.

42. On the right side of the Fusion, press O (the

letter O, not zero), then 7 to select the sound R&B
Kit.

43. As you did with the bass track, scroll down to the
Arp Num, and change the value. Being that this is a
third pattern in a single song, we will set the Arp
Num to 3.

44. Check to make sure the ARP ON/OFF button is
bright, then press a key to see if the Simple Drone
plays back. If it does, we're ready to set an arp.

45. Press the soft button labeled Arp.

46. At the top of the screen, scroll to EDIT Arp and
set the value to Arp 3.

47. Scroll down and set the Pattern to ROM: Drum
Patterns.

48.Scroll down and change A-1 (000) to P-5 (1 24)
R&B 3. (Note: It may take you a long time to get
there as it is the 124th pattern in the system. To get
there fast, use the control wheel and scroll clockwise
at a moderate speed to save time.)

49. Press and hold the middle C key. You should
hear the drum pattern R&B 3 play.

50. Press RECORD, then PLAY. Record eight
measures. When finished, press STOP.

That's it! You've just recorded a full piano, bass and
drum track quickly, easily, and with barely any
effort!

The Fusion has literally hundreds of arp's built in. Combine this with the fact the Fusion has many super-quality sounds at your disposal, and you'll be making music faster than you ever thought possible.

Using the sequencer with audio and synth together

If you've been asking yourself "Why aren't there on-board multitrack audio recorders in other synthesizer workstations?" The answer is because Alesis (as of this writing in January 2007) is the only one that even offers it.

Some important words about multitrack audio recording with the Fusion

Use a mixing board

When recording any audio, it is highly suggested (but not required) that you run your instrument(s) through a proper mixing board, then to the Fusion. While it's true you can plug in "direct" without a mixer, this may at times lead to undesirable results. Alesis themselves makes audio mixing boards you can use that will work wonderfully with the Fusion. You can find suitable mixers of all ranges (including some with very reasonable prices) at www.alesis.com, or at your local Alesis retailer.

Recording audio is not the Fusion's primary function

Bear in mind that the multitrack audio recording ability of the Fusion is not its primary function. The Fusion is an instrument first. It is not designed to replace a full recording studio. This is not to say you couldn't mix and master an entire album on it, but you should know where the Fusion's priorities are.

It still takes time to get recorded audio to sound good

Recording physical audio with the Fusion is convenient, but not necessarily make the process any faster. As is the case with true recording studios, you will still have to spend time setting up microphone placement, tuning instruments and the like.

The quality of the output is 100% dependent on the quality of the input

If you feed the Fusion crappy audio, you will get crappy audio in return. While the Fusion does produce clean pristine sounds on the synthesizer end, it will not magically turn a crappy audio recording into a good one. In essence, you will have to make an effort to make sure the audio you send is good from the start. This isn't to say your audio "must be perfect", but rather that your audio must be as clean as you can get it.

If you do not use amplification, the signal may be too "weak" to use

You can adjust audio volume levels once something is recorded into the Fusion, but it helps a great deal if you have some amplification (hence the suggestion of using a mixing board) when recording audio.

Example of an instrument that works "as is": Acoustic-Electric guitar with powered pickup. Most acoustic-electric guitars come provided with a 9-volt battery that allows for amplification when sending audio out. This is a good strong signal and will work well with the Fusion.

Instruments that will not work: Electric guitars and non-powered microphones. The electric guitar itself has no amplification, and therefore will have a weak signal. A non-powered microphone has the same problem.

For non-powered instruments, using a mixing board (whereas you can increase the volume a great deal) will help immensely.

Recording your first song with synth + audio

1. Create a new song on the Fusion and record eight measures. I recommend creating a simple drum track, even if it is something simple such as hi-hat tapping.

2. Press the SONG button.

3. Press the EDIT button.

4. Press the soft button labeled Song.

5. Press the soft button labeled Add Track.

6. Use your INC and DEC buttons or the control wheel to change Synth to Audio.

7. Press the soft button labeled OK.

   A new track will be created, entitled Audio Track 1. Note: Even if the actual track is track 2, the title of the track will still be Audio Track 1.

8. Physically plug an instrument into Audio Input 1, located on the back of the Fusion.

9. Press the soft button labeled Song.

10. You will see at the bottom of the screen Track 2: no signal.

11. Physically play the instrument plugged into

Audio Input 1. You should see some activity on your screen indicating the Fusion can "hear" the instrument being played. If you do not any activity, no signal is being sent to the Fusion.

12. Press LOCATE and REW to return to the beginning of the song.

13. Press RECORD.

14. Press PLAY.

15. Record a few measures with the instrument plugged into the Fusion.

16. When finished, press STOP.

17. Press LOCATE and REW to return to the beginning of the song.

18. Press PLAY. You should hear your newly recorded audio along with your synth track.

Adjusting audio track settings

To modify settings for an audio track:

1. Press the SONG button.

2. Press the EDIT button.

3. Press the soft button labeled Track.

4. Press the soft button labeled General.

5. Highlight EDIT Track using the INC and DEC buttons or the control wheel.

Things you cannot edit with an audio track

Range. This is an audio track and therefore doesn't apply to the keyboard at all.

Param. Again, applies to the keyboard. You cannot transpose an audio track as it is not a playable keyboard sound.

Controls. Once again, keyboard specific, and therefore disabled as it does not apply to an audio track.

The Output screen is the one you will want to pay most attention to. After selecting the audio track, you can press the soft button labeled Output to get there.

In this area, you can modify volume, pan, apply effects buses, and so on. Modify to your liking.

Giving your audio tracks extra volume

Note: This is not to be confused with the Output screen. You can give your tracks additional volume by directly adjusting the recorded file itself. Here's how to do it.

Let's say you recorded an audio track on track 2...

1. Press the SONG button.

2. Press the EDIT button.

3. Press the soft button labeled Editor.

4. Using the PREV and NEXT buttons, highlight track 2.

5. Use the INC and DEC buttons or the control wheel to place a check in the box for track 2.

6. Make sure that no other tracks are selected.

   IMPORTANT NOTE: If your song has over six tracks, the Fusion will display six tracks at a time on this screen. To view tracks 7 and up, you will need to use the PREV and NEXT buttons to highlight the field next to View Tracks, and then use the INC and DEC buttons or the control wheel to the additional tracks, if your song has more than six tracks to it.

7. Press the soft button labeled Process.

8. Use the NEXT and PREV buttons to highlight the field next to Process.

9. Use the INC and DEC buttons or the control wheel to select Audio Gain.

10. Use the NEXT and PREV buttons to select Edit Start, then set the time for the edit to start (usually the beginning of the song). Then select Edit End and set the the time for the edit to end.

Note: For most audio tracks, you will most likely want to adjust gain on the entire track. When you are selecting an Edit Start time, roll the control wheel counterclockwise until the start point reads 001:01.000. When you are selecting the Edit End time, roll the control wheel clockwise. The number will increase and then eventually stop. Where it stops is the where the song ends.

11. Use the PREV and NEXT buttons to highlight the field next to Gain, which should currently read +0 dB.

12. If you want to INCREASE volume, set the value as a positive number. If you want to DECREASE the volume, set the value as a negative number.

13. When ready to apply the gain, press the soft button labeled Execute. The Fusion will

report "Applying Gain". This will take some time as it is directly affecting a recorded file. Shorter lengths of time will obviously process faster than longer ones.

Tips for what amount of dB to increase or decrease

If you're not sure what to use for a dB value, a good rule of thumb is to use +3 dB or -3 dB to start with. In most instances, this will not make your audio too "hot" or too "weak". If after applying the audio gain you are still not satisfied with the result, add or subtract another 3 dB.

When you become familiar with what works for you, you will know in the future what to set for the audio gain.

When is too much too much?

If you have increased the volume too much, you will hear digital clipping, meaning the sound will have sharp digital sounds that are very undesirable.

If you have decreased the volume too much, you will hear what is best described as phasing. The audio will have lost too much clarity due to gain reduction and sound like a bad connection on a phone line.

Does "Undo" work if I make a mistake?

NO. Pressing UNDO will not remove a previous audio gain edit when editing an audio track. This is why it's highly suggested that when you are applying gains to increase or decrease no more than 3 dB until you become comfortable with what gains work for you.

Fusion Convertor how-tos

These how-to's are for the Microsoft Windows XP version only. There is a Macintosh version, but I did not have an Apple Macintosh computer available for documenting at the time this book was written. It is assumed the Mac version operates the same way as the Windows version.

Q: What is the Fusion Converter?

A: An application (software) that allows you to literally convert sample to Alesis Fusion format.

Q: Does the Fusion Converter record sound?

A: No. It only converts existing samples.

Q: Where do I get the Fusion Converter?

A: Go to the www.alesis.com web site, click the "Support" link, then "Downloads", then "Software/Drivers", then "FUSION 6HD / 8HD". The Fusion Converter is bundled as a ZIP file.

How do I install the Fusion Converter after downloading it?

If you want to know where to download the Fusion Converter from, see the previous section.

Extract the installation program from the downloaded ZIP file. If using WinZip (available at www.winzip.com), when you double-click the file, you should see something like this:

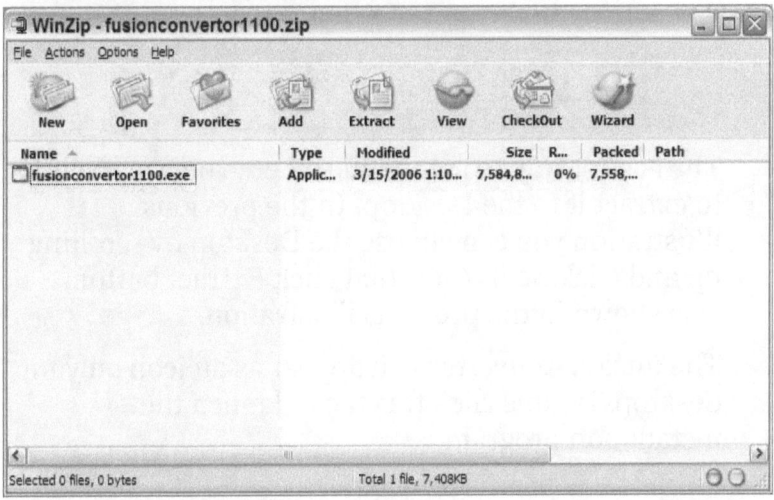

Press the Extract button. You should then see this:

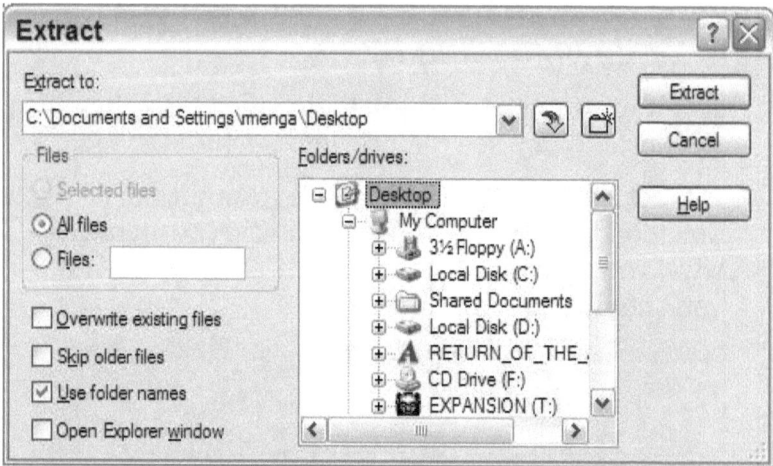

The easiest way to get the file where you can see it is to extract it to the Desktop. In the previous illustration you can choose the Desktop by scrolling up and clicking it. After that click Extract button, also shown in the previous illustration.

The Fusion Converter will appear as an icon on your desktop. Double click this file to launch the installation program.

Each screen of the installation program will look like this:

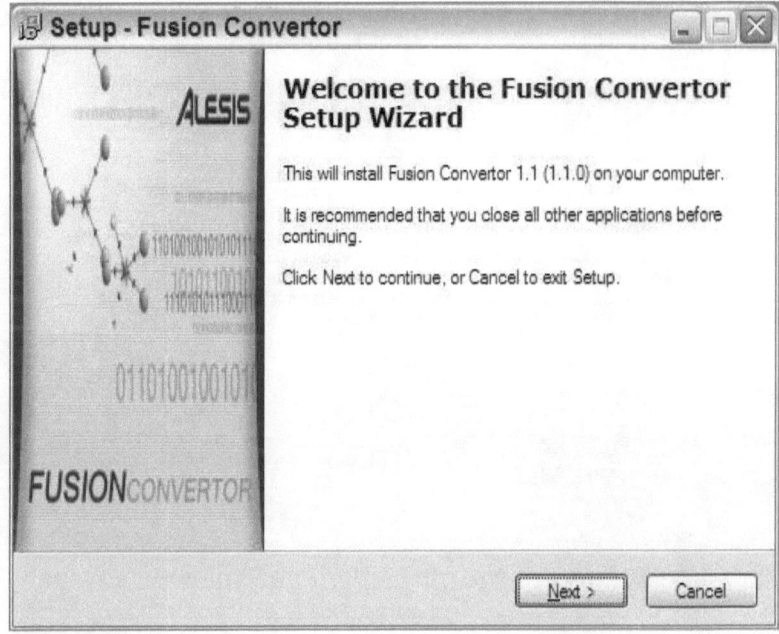

Click *Next*

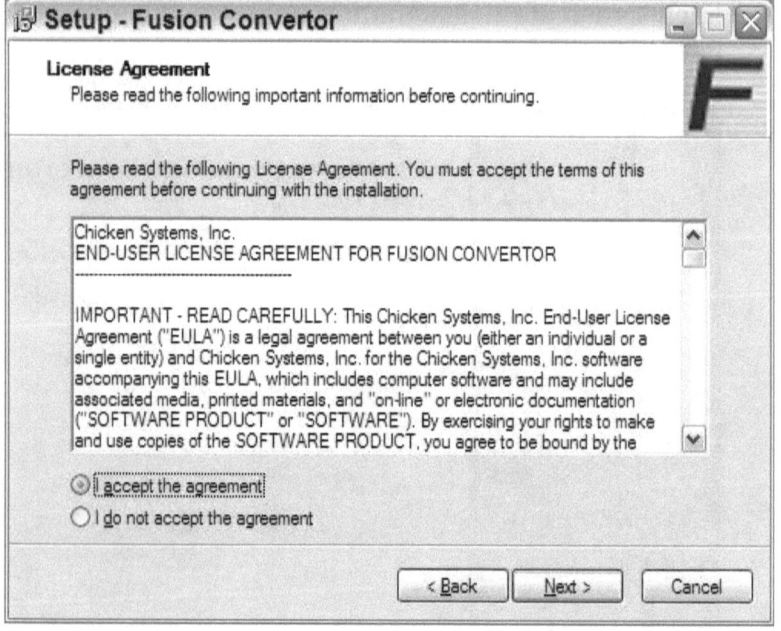

Choose *I accept the agreement* and then click *Next*

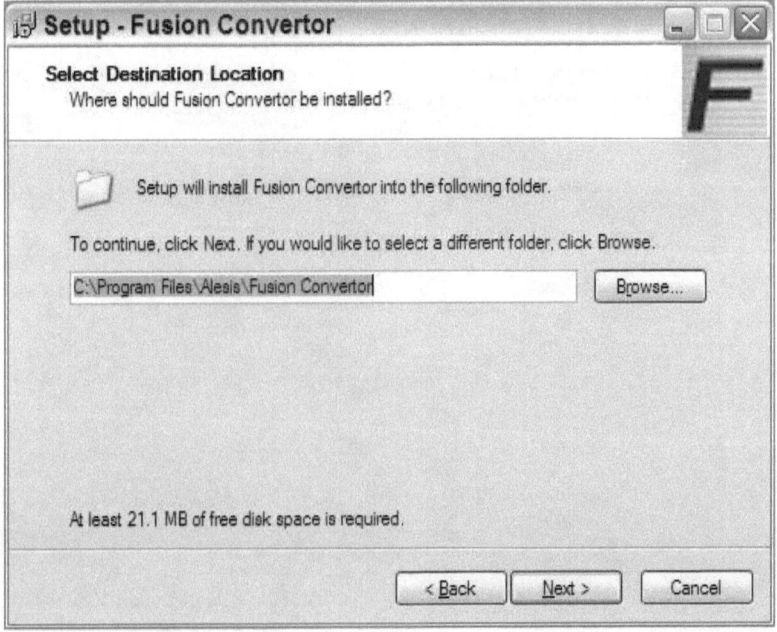

Click *Next*

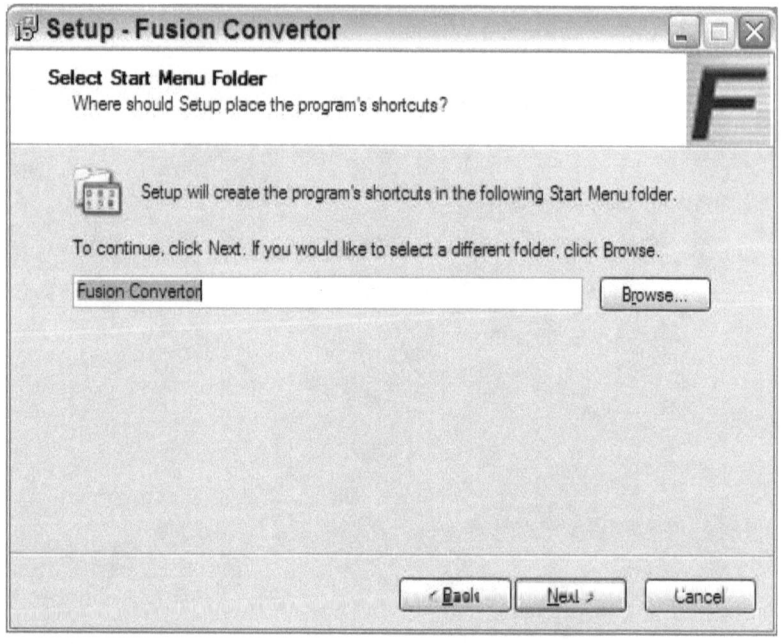

Click *Next*

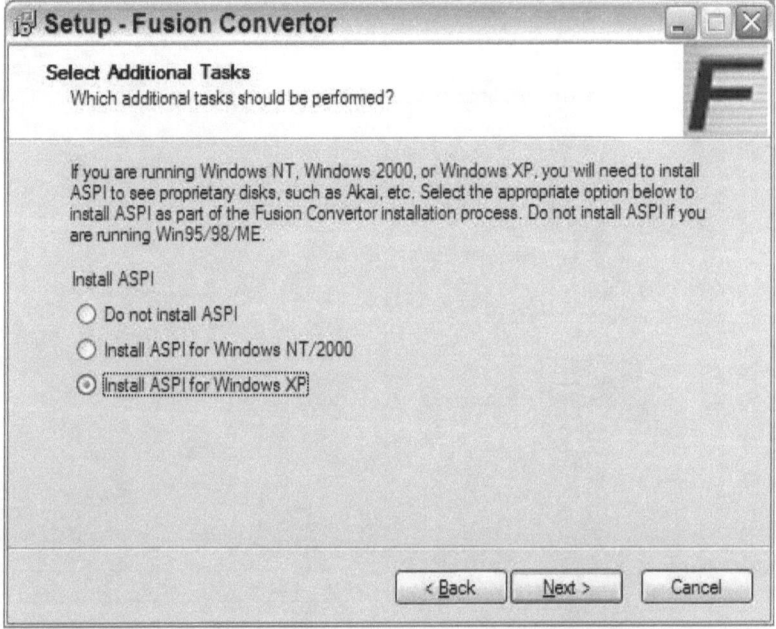

Choose *Install ASPI for Windows XP* and click *Next*

Note: If you are using Windows NT or Windows 2000, choose *Install ASPI for Windows NT/2000* instead.

Are you running Microsoft Windows 98? I was not able to test this software with Windows 98. I am assuming it would install, but do not know if it would actually work afterward.

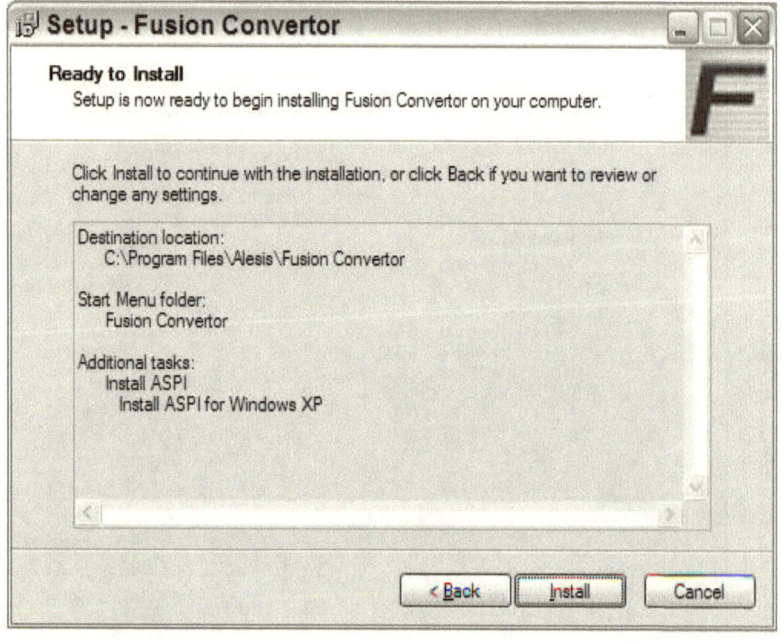

Click *Install*

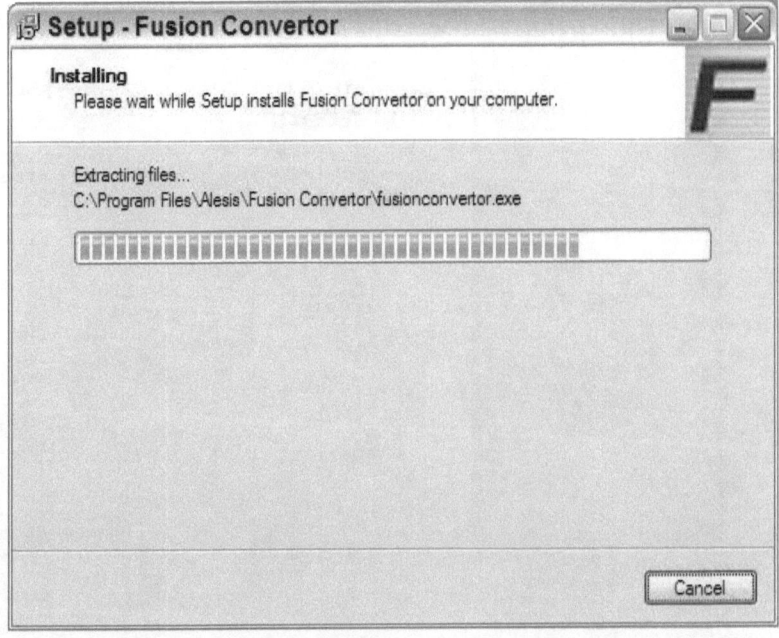

The application will install. Wait until finished.

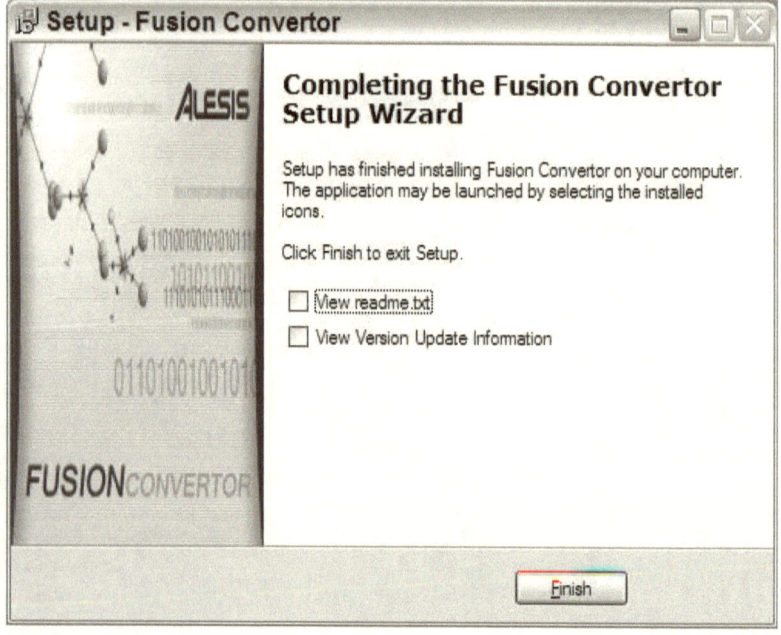

Click *Finish*

The Fusion Converter at this point is installed. The
program can be launched from Start button, All
Programs, Fusion Convertor, Alesis, Fusion
Convertor, and would look similar to this:

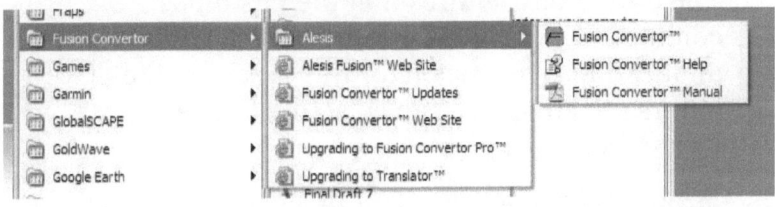

Preparing the Fusion for computer use before launch the Converter

The Converter requires that the Fusion be connected via USB before you launch the application. The reason for this is so that the drive letters are already assigned so the Converter can locate them easily.

Windows XP does not require any drivers to be installed for the Fusion to detect properly.

All drives from the Fusion will be detected automatically.

Getting to know the Fusion Converter

The initial first screen after launching the Fusion
Converter looks like this:

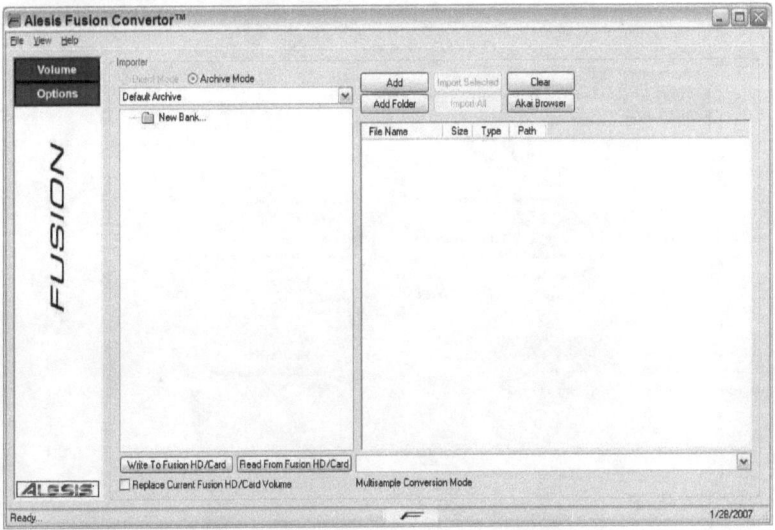

This is the Volume screen.

To the top left are two buttons labeled Volume and Options, and yes, these are buttons although they don't look like them. If you click Volume, nothing happens because you are already on the Volume screen. If you click Options, this is what happens:

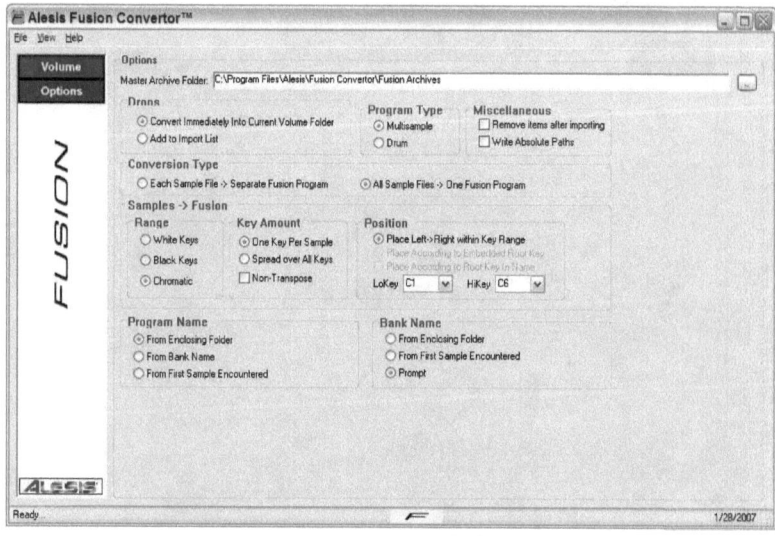

Setting your options first

While on the Options screen, here is an explanation of the areas to pay attention to:

Master Archive Folder

This is located at the very top of the Options screen. The default location is C:\Program Files\Alesis\Fusion Convertor\Fusion Archives. You can change this location if you like.

Drops

This is a poorly written way of saying "How to handle Drag 'n' Drops", meaning if you click a WAV file, drag it to the Converter application and drop it in there, how should the application treat it? This should be left as Convert Immediately Into Current Volume Folder.

Program Type

Unless you are specifically programming a drum kit, this should be left as Multisample.

Miscellaneous

Leave both these options unchecked.

Conversion Type

If set to Each Sample File -> Separate Fusion Program, each sample imported into the Converter will be played as a separate program once sent to the Fusion, with each program utilizing all the keys on the keyboard. For example, if you send a sample of a dog barking and a bird chirping, these samples will be selectable separately. When you select the dog barking, the middle C key will play the sample as originally recorded. When you play keys lower or higher than middle C, the pitch will be different.

If set to All Sample Files -> One Fusion Program, every sample you import will be sent to the Fusion as a single program, with a different sample assigned to each key.

If this sounds confusing already, don't worry. I will provide an example of what to use in a moment.

Range

White keys = use nothing but white keys

Black keys = use nothing but black keys

Chromatic = use both black and white keys

Key Amount

One key per sample = One keyboard key plays the sample

Spread over all the keys = All keys are available to play a sample

Non-Transpose = If checked, the sample played will not adjust pitch

Position

It is suggested to leave as is, with *Place Left -> Right within Key Range* as the selected option, LoKey as C1 and HiKey as C6.

Program Name

These options will only be available if you have All Sample Files -> One Fusion Program from Conversion Type. It is suggested, if these options are available to you, to select *From Enclosing Folder*.

Bank Name

It is suggested to have this set to *From Enclosing Folder*

Suggested Options for easiest use with SOUND EFFECTS

IMPORTANT NOTE: These are suggested settings. You will have to experiment to see what works best for you when importing samples to the Fusion.

From the Options screen:

Program Type	Multisample
Miscellaneous	Both options unchecked
Conversion Type Separate	Each Sample File → Fusion Program
Range	White Keys
Key amount	Spread over All Keys
Non-Transpose	Unchecked
Position Key	Place Left → Right within Range
LoKey	C1
HiKey	C6
Program Name	N/A using these options
Bank Name	From Enclosing Folder

Suggested Options for easiest use with CHROMATIC SOUNDS

IMPORTANT NOTE: These are suggested settings. You will have to experiment to see what works best for you when importing samples to the Fusion.

From the Options screen:

Program Type	Multisample
Miscellaneous	Both options unchecked
Conversion Type Fusion	All sample files → One Program
Range	Chromatic
Key amount	Spread over All Keys
Non-Transpose	Unchecked
Position Key	Place Left → Right within Range
LoKey	C1
HiKey	C6
Program Name	From Enclosing Folder
Bank Name	From Enclosing Folder

Importing sound effect WAV samples

Now that we've set our options, it's time to import some samples.

If you used the suggested options above for sound effects, you will notice I purposely have From Enclosing Folder used for the Bank Name. This means that the folder my WAV samples are located in will be the name of the bank itself.

Preparing a folder

If I have a set of WAV samples I want to use as a sound bank, this is what I do:

1. Create a folder called ALESIS under the My Documents folder.

2. Create a sub-folder under ALESIS to whatever I want the name of the bank to be.

For example, if I want to have some Monty Python
sound effects, I create a folder called Monty Python
under ALESIS, then place my WAV samples there. It
looks like this:

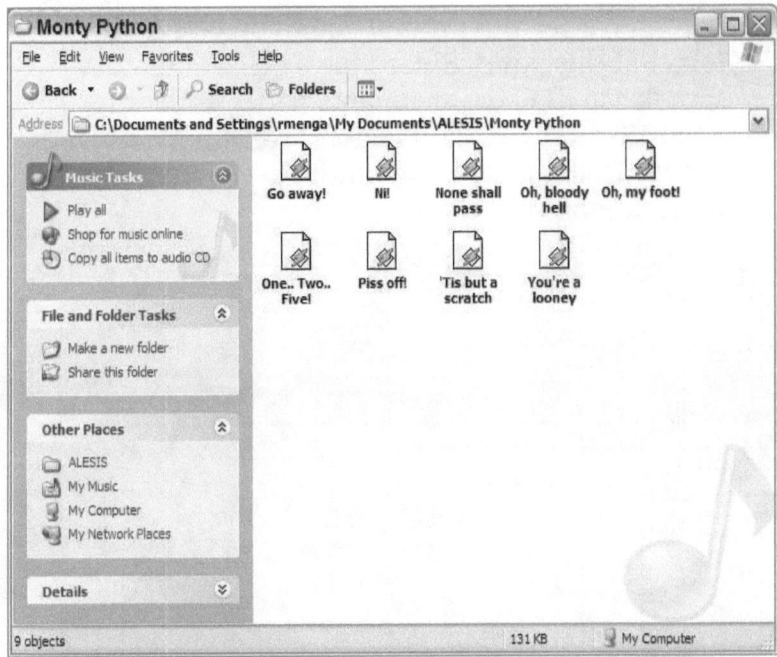

After I have placed all the WAV samples I want to import, I go back to the Fusion Converter and press the Volume button at the top left. Then I click Add Folder.

The Converter will prompt you to browse for a folder at this point. Since I have placed my WAV samples in the My Documents folder under the ALESIS\Monty Python folder, I can simple expand the My Documents folder until I get to the one I want. It looks like this:

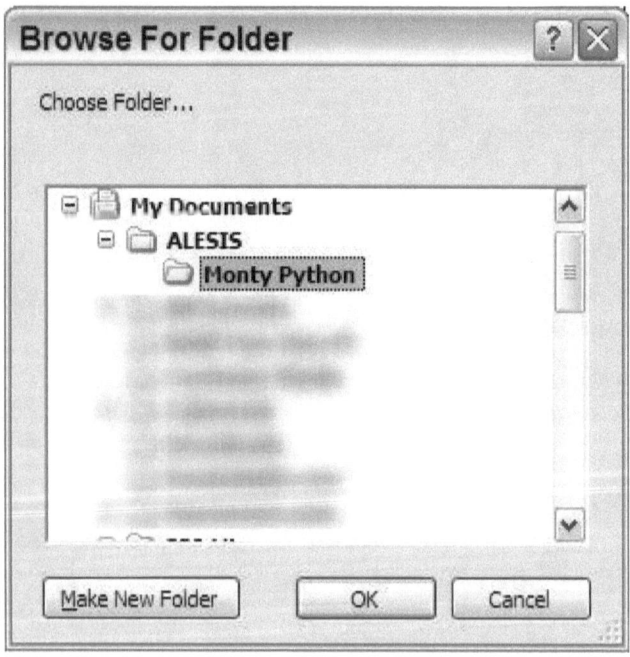

After I have my folder selected, I click OK. Back in
the Converter, the Volume screen now looks like
this:

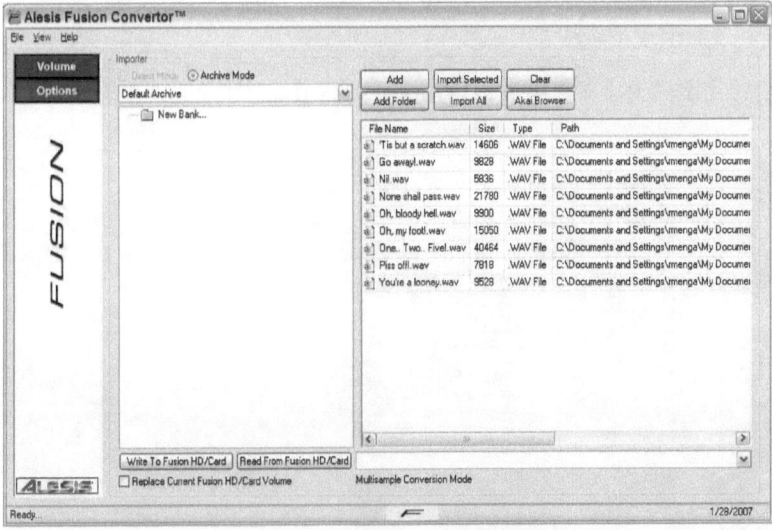

As shown above, all my WAV samples have been
successfully imported into the Fusion Converter.

Now it's time to convert the sounds.

Press the button labeled Import All.

If successful, the Converter will report *Importing Completed!*

The Volume screen now looks like this:

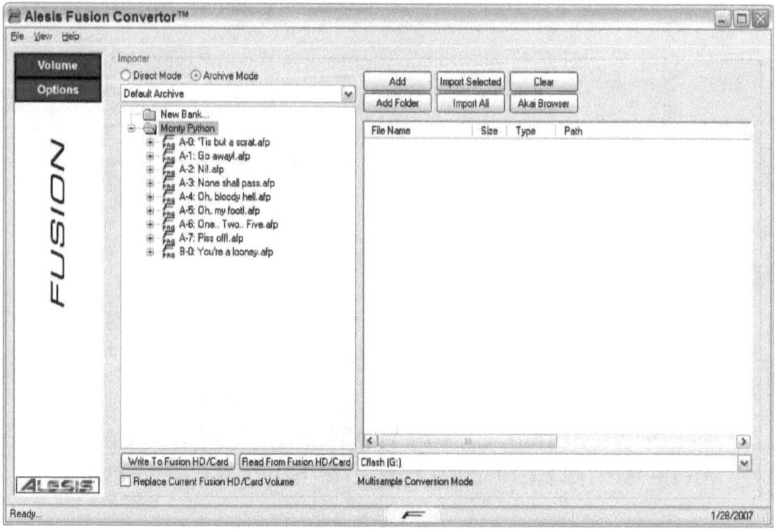

IMPORTANT NOTE: Did you get an error on attempt to import? It was most likely because the WAV sample rate too low to be imported to the Fusion.

If you attempt to convert 8-bit sample rate WAV files, THIS WILL NOT WORK. The Fusion requires the WAV samples to be a minimum of 16-bit. Mono files (even at

11025kHz) are OKAY, but they must be a minimum of 16-bit.

Free software is available for Windows and Mac to convert sample rates if that's what you need to do. I suggest using Audacity. This can be downloaded from http://audacity.sourceforge.net. Refer to Audacity's documentation on how to convert sample rates.

Note that the Bank Name at the top is called Monty Python. It is called this because the folder the WAV's came from was literally titled Monty Python , and the option in the Converter was set to use From Enclosing Folder for the Bank Name.

Now that we have converted samples ready to send, let's send them to the Fusion.

At the bottom right of the Converter on the Volume screen, I choose my Fusion's hard drive. On my computer, it is assigned as drive letter H, and is labeled Fusion Hd. Your drive letter may be different, but the label should still be Fusion Hd.

This is what it looks like from the Volume screen in the Converter:

IMPORTANT NOTE: You optionally have the ability to write to the Fusions CF (CompactFlash) card if there is one installed instead of the Fusion's hard drive itself. However, it's recommended that your CF is formatted properly by the Fusion before sending any samples to it. If you have been following this book from the beginning, you've already formatted your CF properly. If not, refer to the section Installing and Formatting your CF card earlier in this book.

ALSO NOTE: Samples loaded to the CF card will load more slowly compared to the hard drive. This is because the transfer speed of a CF is much slower compared to a hard drive. If you find that your Fusion "thinks a lot" when loading samples from the CF, this is not a flaw in the Fusion. It's a limitation of the CF transfer speed itself.

When ready click the button in the Converter labeled Write to Fusion HD/Card. The Converter will write the samples to the Fusion, and then report when it is finished.

At this point you can Safely Remove Hardware in

Windows XP. Instructions are provided how to do
this previously in this book in the section Download
and extract the sounds from hollowsun.com. Refer
to that section for instructions.

Some additional words

Always use Safely Remove Hardware when you unmount drives from Windows

Unplugging your Fusion without using the Safely Remove Hardware method first is not recommended, as it can potentially corrupt the files on the Fusion!

Is it required to "Verify" after sending sounds or samples using the Converter?

No. Compared to imported HollowSun.com sounds, using the Fusion Converter does not require any additional steps once the sounds are sent to the Fusion. Once you unmount the Fusion properly from Windows XP (see above), the sounds will be ready to select via the BANK buttons or CATEGORY button, just like when you're selecting built-in sounds.

How do I <u>remove</u> sounds and/or samples I've previously sent to the Fusion?

In my experience, the best way to remove sounds and/or samples is to do it manually via the Windows Explorer (not to be confused with Internet Explorer; that's a web browser). While this may sound like a daunting task at first, it's actually quite easy considering each bank has it's own folder.

This process requires you to do two things:

1. Manually edit bank.txt files using Windows Notepad.

2. Carefully remove folders from the Fusion's Hard Drive (or CF if you put them there). Again, this sounds very complicated – but it's not.

Earlier in this book, we installed the Hollow Sun Freepack #1. Now we'll uninstall them.

Select a stock pre-installed sound, such as Holy
Grail Grand Piano. Your display should look like
this (we do this so after you do not receive a "sound
not found" error after uninstallation):

PROGRAM

		Synth:	Sample
[ROM: PRESET 1]	**A-1 (000)**	Cat:	Piano

Holy Grail Grand Piano

Tempo:	128.0
MIDI Chan:	1
Transpose:	0

1:Master EQ 2:Master EQ 3:Bus1 Para... 4:Bus2 Send*

Plug in the USB cable to the Fusion, and then to
your computer.

Bring up the Windows Explorer by clicking Start, All
Programs, Accessories, Windows Explorer.

Expand the Volume folder and highlight
Multisamples. Within this folder will be a file called
bank.txt, or possibly just bank. It will look like this:

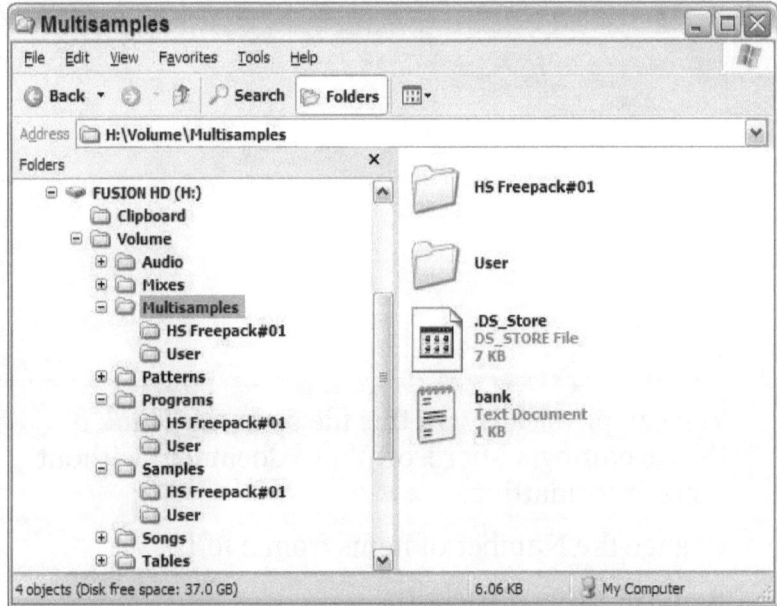

Note that the Multisamples folder is highlighted,
and the files within that folder are on the right pane.

Double-click the bank file. It will look like this:

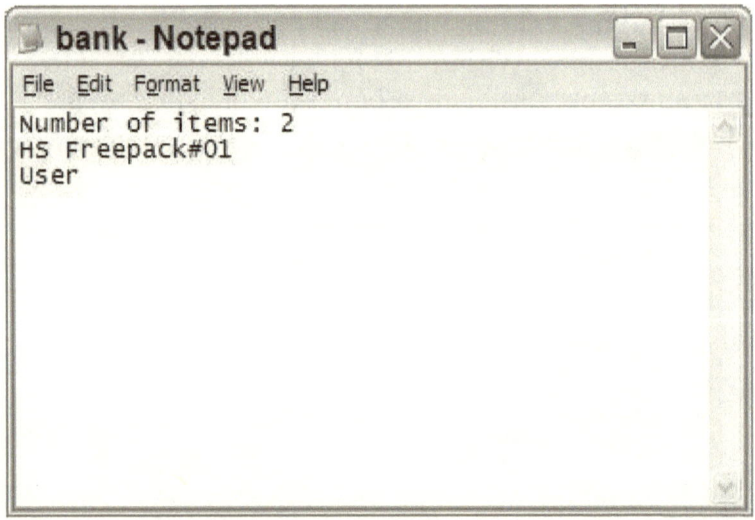

You can physically edit this file by hand. Think of this as editing a Microsoft Word document without fonts or formatting.

Change the Number of items from 2 to 1.

Remove HS Freepack#01.

When done, it should look like this:

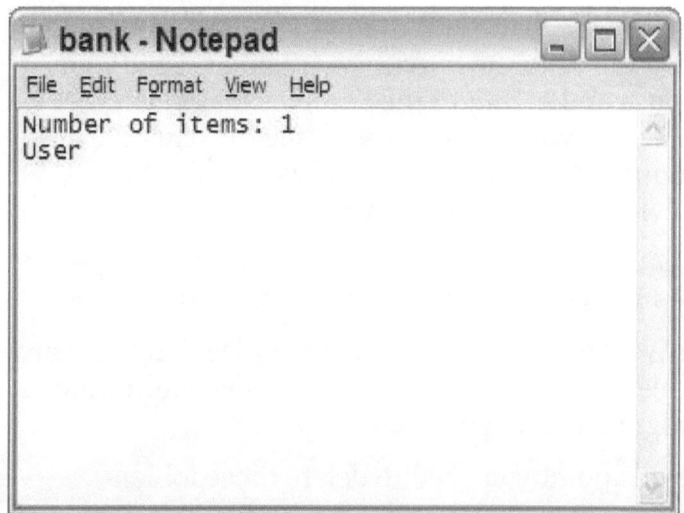

Close Notepad. You will be asked if you want to save the file. Click Yes to save.

There are two more bank.txt files you need to edit. They look exactly like the one we just edited and saved. All you have to do is edit to make them all look the same.

The two other files are located in the folders Programs and Samples.

Back in Windows Explorer, you will still have the Multisamples folder highlighted. Take your mouse and highlight the Programs folder. On the right side you will once again see the bank file. Double-click it, edit it exactly as you did the previous one, exit and save.

Once again, back in Windows Explorer, you now have the Programs folder highlighted. Take your mouse and highlight the Samples folder. On the right side you will once again see the bank file. Double-click it, edit it exactly as you did the previous one, exit and save.

If you've gotten this far, you've officially completed step 1 of removing the sounds. Step 2 is very easy.

In Windows Explorer, you will notice that there are three HS Freepack#01 folders, under Multisamples, Programs and Samples.

At this point you need to delete those folders.

FOLLOW THESE INSTRUCTIONS VERY SLOWLY AND VERY CAREFULLY TO AVOID DELETING FUSION DATA ACCIDENTALLY.

SINGLE RIGHT CLICK the HS Freepack#01 folder
under the folder Multisamples, like this:

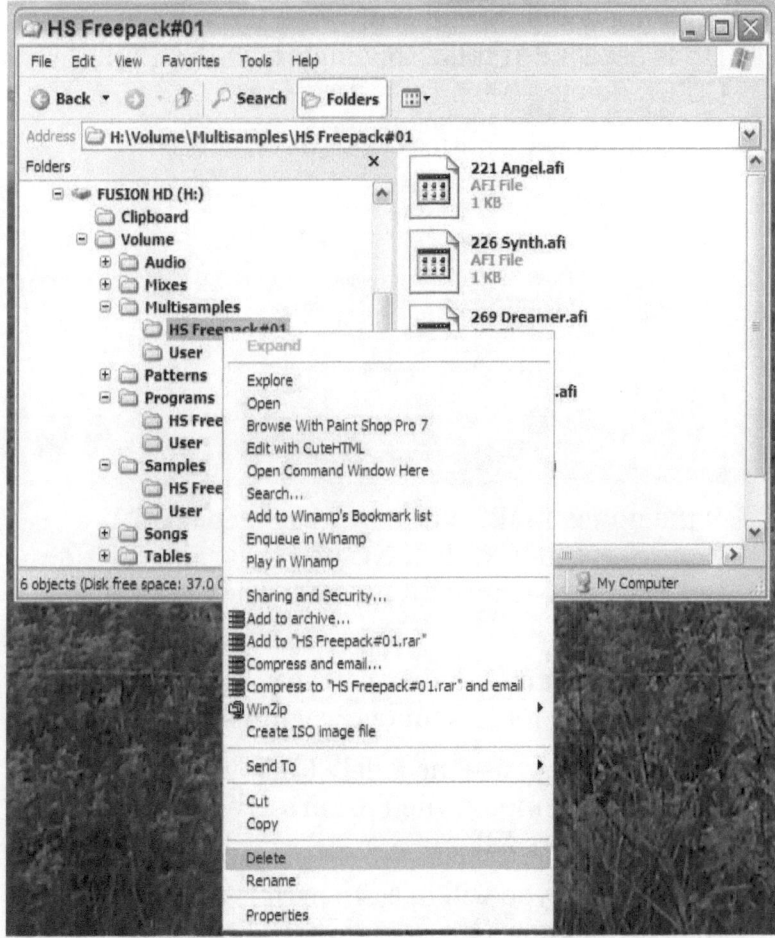

IT IS VERY IMPORTANT that the HS Freepack#01

folder is highlighted, AND NOT THE
MULTISAMPLES FOLDER ITSELF.

Once you have absolute confirmation you have the
HS Freepack#01 folder highlighted, SINGLE LEFT
CLICK delete.

You should get a notice that looks like this:

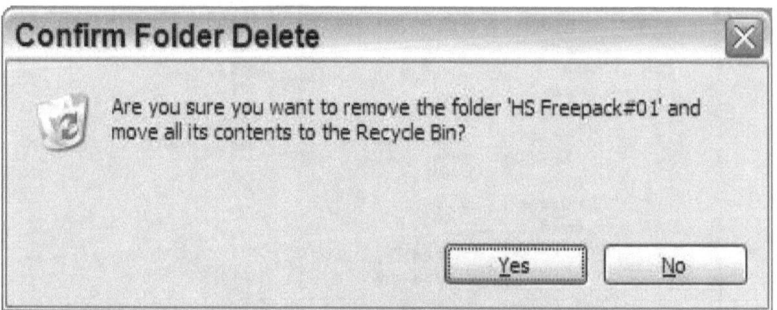

If the notice DOES NOT say 'HS Freepack#01'
somewhere in it, CLICK NO and try again. If it does
say 'HS Freepack#01', it is safe to click Yes and
delete.

Repeat this same process for the other two HS
Freepack#01 folders under Programs and Samples.

When finished, use the Safely Remove Hardware
method to unmount the Fusion's drive(s) safely
from Windows XP.

At this point you will need to perform a "Verify" so
the Fusion knows the sounds have been deleted.
Follow the same procedure to verify as you were

instructed to when originally installing the HS Freepack#01 earlier in this book, and then the sounds and its Fusion references will be completed removed.

These uninstall instructions will work for any additional sounds you place into the Fusion from the Hollow Sun web site that you want to remove later.

What happens if I load a song that uses a sound that isn't in my Fusion anymore?

The Fusion will report that the sound it needs doesn't exist when the song loads, and it will substitute the sound with something else (usually Holy Grail Grand Piano). It will not cause the Fusion to crash.

2019 update for related web links

As stated in the introduction, this is the part of the book that lists internet resources that as of 2019 are still online and available.

FUSIONEER FORUMS

http://fusioneer.proboards.com/

ALESIS FUSION REFERENCE MANUAL, FUSION CONVERTOR AND HOLLOW SUN DOWNLOADS

https://yamahamusicians.com/forum/viewforum.php?f=155

The End!

I hope you've found the information helpful in this book – and I also wish you the best of success with your music making.

Remember, composing on a synthesizer workstation is unlike using any other instrument. It is a combination of art and technology. You are the artist; the one who creates the music. The Fusion is the technology, allowing you to bring your ideas to fruition.

The workstation synthesizer is only used by the select few capable of putting the art and technology together to create wonderful music. With the Fusion, you are one step ahead by having one of the most powerful synths available to do the task.

Enjoy it.